𝔖uperstition!

Also by Willard A. Heaps
Assassination: A Special Kind of Murder
Birthstones
Long Journeys: Stories of Human Endurance
Riots, U.S.A.
The Story of Ellis Island
Taxation, U.S.A.
Wall of Shame
Wandering Workers: The Story of American Migrant Farm Workers and Their Problems

With Porter W. Heaps
The Singing Sixties: The Spirit of Civil War Days Drawn from the Music of the Times

SUPERSTITION!

Willard A. Heaps

THOMAS NELSON INC.
Nashville • Camden • New York

Copyright © 1972 by Willard A. Heaps

All rights reserved under International and Pan-American Conventions. Published in Nashville, Tennessee, by Thomas Nelson Inc. and simultaneously in Don Mills, Ontario, by Thomas Nelson & Sons (Canada) Limited. Manufactured in the United States of America.

First edition

Library of Congress Cataloging in Publication Data
Heaps, Willard Allison, date
  Superstition!

  SUMMARY: Examines the origins, persistence, and bases, if any, for superstitions concerning sports, medicine, weather, music, theater, marriage, and other areas.
  Bibliography: p.
  1. Superstition—Juvenile literature. [1. Superstition] I. Title.
  BF1775.H4   001.9'6   72-8114
  ISBN 0-8407-6226-7

Contents

1	The Tenacity of Superstition	9
2	Some Who Believed	22
3	Are You Superstitious?	34
4	Unfounded Beliefs	45
5	A Little Bit of Luck	53
6	Sports and Superstition	71
7	Superstition in the Worlds of Music and the Theater	82
8	Foretelling the Future	98
9	Predicting the Weather	108
10	Superstitions of the Sea	122
11	Folk Medicine	133
12	Love and Courtship	142
14	Marriage	154
15	Death	170
	Appendix	190
	Sources and Readings	192
	Index	198

Superstition!

1. The Tenacity of Superstition

> "There is in superstition a senseless fear of God."
> —Cicero, Roman orator, *De natura deorum* (44 B.C.)

Supersitition! The word immediately suggests the magic and sorcery of primitive times—the calling up or exorcising of spirits; the use of incantations, charms, and spells; black magic; the evil eye; witches, demons, and vampires; and practices such as voodooism, necromancy, and fetishism.

It also brings to mind sayings and rhymes that we mutter today in certain situations or use to make decisions, to bring good luck, or to avoid misfortune. Many of these sayings have to be accompanied by rituals or acts intended to make them effective. All of them supposedly lead to a life of contentment, security, and happiness.

As followed today, these superstitions remain much the same as when they were first put into words in the past. In some cases the reason for the superstition has disappeared and just the memory of it is left to keep it alive.

As a word, "superstition" has a variety of meanings. Derived from the Latin *superstitio,* from *superstare,* which means to stand over (*super,* over; *stare,* to stand), the etymological meaning is "standing over a thing in amazement or awe" *(Oxford English Dictionary).* From this somewhat vague beginning came the interpretations given in various dictionaries. For example, in *Webster's Third New International Dictionary,* the first of three definitions is: "a belief ... or practice resulting from ignorance, unreasoning fear of the unknown or ... trust in magic or chance. ..." All dictionaries emphasize the main quality of superstition—that it is based on fear or ignorance. The fear is of the unknown elements that may influence one's situation or behavior.

Superstition is closely related to magic, to the idea that man can use supernatural forces to control the natural world. Primitive man existed at a time when the forces of nature influenced his everyday life. He did not understand anything about the earth and sky or about the elements that affected him, such as heat and cold, dark and light, or clear and stormy weather. He stood in awe of these things and attributed them to unseen powers, which he came to fear.

Today, in spite of the comfort religion may give us, or our knowledge that everything in nature has a natural cause, some of the feelings of our primitive ancestors remain with us. Irrational fear of what is unknown or mysterious is still widespread.

Many anthropologists refer to superstition as "folk custom or belief." One German encyclopedia on these customs and beliefs runs into ten volumes. Folklorists in England and Scotland have produced scores of volumes of local superstitions. A Japanese volume appeared in 1969; two came from Latin America in 1970; and one each came from India, Italy, and Germany in 1971. More will undoubtedly be published from time to time, for the subject continues to attract investigators.

In the United States collections containing the superstitions of regions and states are published regularly. Wayland D. Hand, director of the Center for the Study of Comparative Folklore and Mythology at the University of California at Los Angeles, is compiling a *Dictionary of American Beliefs and Superstitions,* and has already collected over 400,000 examples. He anticipates finding at least that many more.

During the 1930's, when he was director of the Institute of School Experimentation of Teachers College, Columbia University, Dr. Otis Caldwell studied the superstitious beliefs of eighteen hundred high-school students and published his findings in a book that is still one of the most reliable discussions of the subject in existence. In answering a reporter's question, "Why are people still superstitious today?" Dr. Caldwell offered this concise explanation:

Some superstitions can be traced back to primitive man.

He thought of himself as being in an unfriendly world, and for his own safety he sought friendly powers in the realm of the supernatural. Even during early colonial days our forefathers tried to ward off disease by the use of magic, charms, and incantations. Even though the customs upon which our present-day superstitions were founded have been outgrown in many cases, the superstitions themselves have remained ... for timid people are afraid to abandon them. The truth is we're superstitious only about the things we don't know. When we can't explain why an incident happened, we're too apt to connect it with the supernatural, and to draw conclusions from false evidence and coincidence.

Superstitions are often called half beliefs. Some people accept them implicitly, without examining them to see whether they have any basis in reason or common sense. These people, whether they realize it or not, are truly superstitious. Most of us, however, often go on the assumption that if enough truth seems to exist in a superstition, it is "safer" to obey it. If the superstition concerns good luck, for instance, we might feel that nothing can be lost by paying attention to it. Those who follow the predictions in astrological forecasts may not have complete faith in what the stars and planets are said to foretell, but if past predictions have proved valid often enough, they will accept them.

In all periods of history men have commented both favorably and unfavorably on superstitious belief. Many of them have dismissed superstition as something that involves only the individual person and is harmless to others and therefore tolerable. They maintain that if a

THE TENACITY OF SUPERSTITION

person finds satisfaction and comfort in superstition, he should not be criticized or condemned. Francis Bacon, in his essay "Of Superstition," while considering it to be generally harmful, felt that those who discourage such practices may inflict damage on the believer by taking away the crutch that supports him, however much he is weakened by it. "There is a superstition in avoiding superstition ...," Bacon wrote. "Therefore care would be had that the good be not taken away with the bad, which commonly is done when the person is a reformer."

Nevertheless, critics of superstition often view it as dangerous evidence of insecurity.

In 1822, in an essay called "Popular Superstitions" in *Bracebridge Hall,* Washington Irving discussed the evidences of superstition he found in an English manor house. Of its master, the squire, he wrote, "In his great love for all that is antiquated, he cherishes popular superstitions and listens, with very grave attention, to every tale, however strange." The hall, "with its gloomy galleries and stately chambers adorned with grotesque carvings and faded paintings, produces a state of mind favorable to superstitious fancies."

The author listens to the folktales of goblins and hobgoblins, fairies and ghosts, and curious habits and rituals, then comments,

> These stories are fast fading away, and in another generation or two will probably be completely forgotten. ... There is something, however, about these rural superstitions extremely pleasing to the imagination. The English have given an inexpressible charm to these

beliefs by the manner in which they have associated them with whatever is most homefelt and delightful in nature.

Even now [Irving wrote, when recalling his boyhood] I cannot look upon those fanciful creations of ignorance and credulity without lurking regret that they have all passed away. ... I feel convinced that the true interests and solid happiness of man are promoted by the advancement of truth, yet I cannot but mourn over the pleasant errors which it has transplanted down in its progress.

Although Irving was writing of tales and creatures rather than of guides to action and expectations of good and bad fortune, many modern authorities on child development, not sharing the essayist's belief in the childlike acceptance of such tales, have taken the view that superstition can be dangerous.

Such beliefs, however, do form an important part of childhood, and may be considered distressing only when they are believed by adults. As Irving knew, there is a certain joy in superstitious beliefs, but there is also a danger in them, particularly when they limit the believer's freedom of activity and mislead him with restrictions and fears. This fact explains why superstition has been the target of adverse criticism.

In one of his *Spectator* papers in the early eighteenth century, Joseph Addison described "A Superstitious Household" with which he had dined. Throughout the meal much of the conversation concerned the misfortunes that had either afflicted members of the family or were predicted by them. The mother cited several ill omens and remarked, with a sigh, "My dear, misfortunes never come single." Addison was reproved for spilling salt without throwing a pinch of it over his left shoulder to avoid bad luck, and when he crossed his knife and fork while laying them on his plate at the end of the meal, the hostess urged him to place them side by side lest misfortune come to him.

Since he had not even been aware of the fixed rules he had disregarded, Addison reflected on them after he returned home.

I fell into a profound contemplation on the evils that attend these superstitious follies of mankind [he wrote], how they subject us to imaginary afflictions and additional sorrows that do not properly come within our lot. As if the natural calamities of life were not sufficient for it, we turn the most indifferent circumstances into misfortunes, and suffer as much from trifling accidents as from real evils. I have known the shooting of a star [to] spoil a night's rest, and I have seen a man in love grow pale and lose his appetite upon plucking a merry-thought [a wishbone]. A screech owl at midnight has alarmed a family more than a band of robbers; nay, the voice of a cricket hath struck more terror than the roaring of a lion. There is nothing so inconsiderable that may not appear dreadful to an imagination that is filled with omens.... For my own part, I should be very much troubled were I endowed with this divining quality, even though it should inform me truly of every thing that can befall me. I could not anticipate the relish of any happiness, nor feel the weight of any misery before it actually arises.

The opponents of superstition scoff at what Edmund Burke called "the religion of feeble minds." In at least three instances, two in England and one in the United States, such scoffers have aimed at making superstition the subject of ridicule by publicly defying some of the most popular beliefs, with wide attendant publicity.

The first London Thirteen Club was established by a nucleus of journalists during the 1880's, a time when superstitious belief was particularly rampant in England, and both the daily newspapers and periodical publications were devoting much attention to it. Many prominent people were invited to join the group, including the writer Oscar Wilde, who declined. He assured the founders that much as he would enjoy their company at their dinner gatherings, he loved his superstitions more. "Superstitions are the color element of thought and imagination," he wrote. "They are the opponents of common sense, which is the enemy of romance.... The aim of your society seems to be dreadful. Leave us some unreality. Don't make us too offensively sane."

The seventy-eight members held the club's first dinner on the thirteenth of January, 1884. There were six tables with thirteen diners at each. (Ten years later the number of tables, each seating thirteen, was thirteen.) Each member wore a peacock feather in his buttonhole, because peacock feathers are considered to be very unlucky. When summoned to dinner by the smashing of a large mirror, the members walked into the restaurant's dining room under a ladder. The knives in the place settings were crossed, in defiance of a bad-luck belief, and the waiters were cross-eyed, because cross-eyed persons are thought to possess the power of the evil eye. In defiance of the popular superstition that a pinch of spilled salt should be thrown over the left shoulder to prevent bad luck, a quarrel, or the death of one member at the table, they spilled salt from coffin-shaped saltcellars.

The reaction of the public was as predicted. The majority of the many readers who wrote to *The Times,* for example, were both outraged and worried. Superstition, they maintained, should not be treated as a joke, and such flaunting of established beliefs could only serve to bring misfortune to those guilty of such acts.

The annual dinners of the London Thirteen Club were discontinued in 1897 "because of a lack of interest in the aims of the club." A new London Thirteen Club was not established until the early 1920's, when, after World War I, a renewed wave of interest in superstition seized the English public.

In the United States the first antisuperstition body, which used the impressive name of the National Committee of Thirteen Against Superstition, Prejudice and Fear, was organized on Friday, August 13, 1946. Through good-natured spoofing in public, the members hoped to demonstrate that the most common superstitions were absurd, ridiculous, and without reason, having no basis in fact. The founder, Nick Matsoukas, a motion-picture executive, was fully qualified for such a mission. He was born in Greece on June 13, the thirteenth child in a family of thirteen children. His name contained thirteen letters, and he arrived in the United States as an immigrant on February 13, 1917.

The members met regularly on unlucky Fridays to walk

under ladders, hold black cats, and throw rabbits' feet into trash cans. These well-publicized gatherings took place wherever a large audience could gather—in hotels, on theater stages, and even in museums. At first spectators were awed when committee members lighted three cigarettes on one match, opened umbrellas indoors, and smashed mirrors. But many soon joined in the harmless fun, and the attendant publicity, although tongue-in-cheek, reached many people.

On its second anniversary the committee gained national attention through an exhibition in the American Museum of Natural History in New York City. Opening on Friday, August 13, the demonstration was held daily for thirteen days. To enter the exhibit, one passed under a shelter of open umbrellas beyond which was a giant cake with thirteen lighted candles. Nearby a young man was systematically smashing mirrors with a hammer. Several displays concerning superstition and prejudice, a branch of superstition, served to impress the viewers with the evils of superstition.

However, the satire and frequent spoofs that have since appeared in print have not had much effect on the extraordinary tenacity of half belief. Superstitious notions and customs persist. Some of them are odd or amusing; many are harmless. Even at best, however, such ideas show an uncritical attitude of mind.

One unexamined superstition has to do with the sudden silence that, for no apparent reason, falls upon a group of people while they are talking. Not satisfied that this is an ordinary occurrence, a superstitious person will interpret it by recalling one of at least two beliefs from his store of

THE TENACITY OF SUPERSTITION

folklore. One of these beliefs is that one of those present will die within the year. The reason for that period of time has never been explained—such things seldom are in superstitions. We may even wonder whether, if the silence occurs at a Christmas gathering, one of the guests will die within a week! Another interpretation is that an unseen angel is passing through the room, and the silence occurs so it will not be disturbed.

The most popular version of the "silence" superstition is an example of the completely false and inaccurate explanations that perpetuate a belief. Many Americans believe that if for no apparent cause everyone in a group suddenly seems at a loss for something to say at twenty minutes after the hour, it is because President Abraham Lincoln was shot and died at 8:20 P.M. while attending a performance of *Our Country Cousin* in Ford's Theater in Washington, D.C. The silence, they believe, has occurred automatically ever since through some unexplained supernatural agency.

The truth is that President Lincoln was shot at 10:10 P.M. and did not die until the next morning. Clocks on display in the windows of jewelry stores are set at 8:20 P.M. not as an erroneous indication of the time of his death, but rather to show the hands on the face in balance.

Critics in the religious field, both scholars and clergymen, have spoken in the press and the pulpit against the evils of superstitious belief and have sought to discourage its growth. They have been unsuccessful.

At least one government, Japan's, became alarmed at

the widespread influence of superstition and tried to discourage it. In 1948 a survey by the Education Ministry revealed that belief in astrology, magic charms, and ancient superstitions, such as *Yakudoshi,* or unlucky years, was rampant all over Japan, particularly in rural areas. The study showed that belief in lucky and unlucky days frequently played havoc with the economy. For example, in one village fishermen refused to go out fishing for several days after the birth of a child in the family. In another village the superstitious refused to leave on the seventh, seventeenth, twenty-fifth, and twenty-seventh of the month or to return on the fifth, fifteenth, and twenty-fifth. That Japan's attack on superstition was only mildly effective is evidenced by the current popularity there of fortune-tellers.

Scientists, too, have waged an endless war against superstition and have called attention to the fact that the development of modern science was actually retarded by the heritage of superstitious belief. Professor Albert G. Keller of Yale University, in his *Science of Society,* says, "Science, which we hold to be true and accurate, develops out of what we now believe to be untrue and inexact.... A superstition is really a belief discarded by 'us,' the enlightened, which persists in the minds of the unenlightened, who ought to know better."

Nevertheless, evidence of superstition has even been observed in the scientific environment of the United States' space program. When the spacecraft Vanguard III was being tested in 1958 for future manned flights, it was previewed for the American public on television. A close-up showed a Saint Christopher medal being attached to the missile. The commentator explained that the saint was the patron of travelers, and he called attention to the use of the medal in automobiles. In this dangerous pioneer flight into the unknown, he noted, its purpose was "for divine guidance."

The next day Dr. Charles Kean, rector of the Church of the Epiphany in Washington, D. C., broke into front-page headlines throughout the country with an indignant protest. "Would it have been just as well in the launching of the third and successful Vanguard to have attached a four-leaf clover to the missile somewhere?" A week later the influential Protestant religious periodical *Christian Century* commented editorially under the title "Superstition in the Atomic Age":

> The fact that a symbol or a word is associated with traditional Christianity does not prevent its being used in the most blatantly superstitious manner possible. . . . During the war we were told that many well-meaning people gave Testaments and prayer books to soldiers, not so much that they might be read but that they might ward off bullets. The ultimate irony was when a particular firm put its Testaments within tungsten steel covers so that, when they were carried over the heart, they might ward off bullets. . . .

Needless to say, the first Mercury spacecraft to orbit space was not visibly protected by Saint Christopher!

2. Some Who Believed

> "Life must be a very tricky thing for the superstitious."
> —A. A. Milne, English novelist, *Not That It Matters* (1920)

According to Margaret Mead, the anthropologist, "Superstition has been a part of every civilization's culture." Men have always practiced superstition in some form or other. The primitive savages lived in terror of the forces of nature and feared the spirits they thought dwelt in every tree, rock, and hill. They believed they had to exorcise these evil demons.

As civilizations developed, each had its own unique type of superstitious belief. In classical antiquity, particularly, great interest was attached to beliefs concerning the

SOME WHO BELIEVED

universe and especially the astral bodies. So great and lasting was this interest that astrology later became a more or less independent field of study. Likewise, early magic and divination (auguries from the behavior of animals, the flights of birds, and the examination of their entrails) subsequently led to a preoccupation with sorcery and witchcraft. Today, of course, although witchcraft and black magic are separate fields of study, the general principles of magic still apply to them.

Superstition is no respecter of persons. Throughout history high and low alike have fallen under its spell. Royal personages were slaves to it, and common folk lived in a world of fear. The intelligent and educated shared beliefs with the hopelessly illiterate. In fact, one may well ask, "Has belief in superstition throughout history changed the course of nations? Have leaders acted on their beliefs in such a way as to bring success or failure?" The question is difficult, if not impossible, to answer.

Rulers—kings, queens, princes—and the nobility have often held unfounded beliefs to explain the unknown. The Egyptian pharaohs, the Greek politicians and philosophers, and the Roman emperors were subject to what they believed was the will of the gods, and behaved accordingly. From the days of Mesopotamia onward monarchs and leaders sought the advice of soothsayers and paid scrupulous attention to it, as well as to the signs and omens of the gods, which were exhibited through natural phenomena and various rituals. If misfortune resulted from their actions, the monarchs believed the gods were displeased; if their actions were successful, they felt the gods had shown their approval. In that way they explained everything that happened.

In *The Birth of Britain,* the first volume of his *History of the English-Speaking Peoples,* Winston Churchill cited two excellent examples of natural phenomena that were thought to predict future events.

Almost a hundred years after Julius Caesar's evacuation of Britain, the Roman Emperor Claudius, who wanted to gain a military reputation, was advised to invade the island again. Accordingly, in the year 43, he organized an army of twenty thousand men.

> The soldiers were indignant at the thought of carrying on a campaign outside the limits of the known world [Churchill writes], but nonetheless they resolved to obey their chief's order. Their delay, however, had made their departure late in the season. The first of three divisions was driven back, and they became discouraged, but they plucked up courage because a flash of light rising in the east shot across to the west, the direction in which they were sailing.

They made a successful landing and found no one to oppose them because the Britons had not expected them.

Saxon England was invaded by the Danes (Vikings) from time to time during the first three quarters of the ninth century. The climax came when Alfred the Great, then twenty-two, succeeded his brother King Ethelred in 871. The Danes advanced with great success, and it took almost superhuman effort for the young king to prevent them from completely subjugating his kingdom. Then, in January, 878, a surprising reversal of Alfred's fortunes occurred with a great victory at Ethandun. Eight hundred Danes were killed and, in Churchill's words,

> the spoils of victory included an enchanted banner called the Raven of which it was said "in every battle in which that banner went before them the raven in the middle of the design seemed to flutter as if it were alive if they were going to have victory." On this occasion it did not flutter, but hung listlessly in its silken folds. The event proved that it was impossible for the Danes to win under these conditions.

Superstition seems to have always played a decisive part in wars and military expeditions, when the fate of a nation was at stake. One of the most prominent military leaders of all time, Napoleon Bonaparte, believed firmly in superstition. Baron de Méneval, Napoleon's private secretary, stressed in his memoirs the effect of the general's belief in his lucky star. He wrote,

> It is commonly believed that great men are superstitious. The masses are superstitious themselves, and assume that mighty deeds can be accomplished only by supernatural means, while others cannot forgive great men their superiority and therefore love to ascribe to them belittling human weaknesses.

Although Napoleon sincerely believed that mysterious and unknown powers controlled his destiny, the baron pointed out, that belief was very different from "the coarse and lower superstitions which place faith in prophecies and the powers of soothsayers, astrologers and other miracle workers." Instead, Napoleon was convinced that he was a providential instrument chosen to carry out an important mission, and that his mystical destiny led him on from success to success. Like every man, he possessed certain weaknesses, and his was an inclination to interpret casual circumstances and peculiar coincidences as indications that he had been chosen by a higher power to accomplish great things.

Napoleon believed that his actions were governed by the occult influence of his guiding star. He even claimed that he saw his personal star shine before him during some of his great victories.

General Jean Rapp, who for a long period was Napoleon's aide-de-camp, referred to this star in his memoirs. He had just returned from the siege of Danzig in 1814, he wrote, and found the Emperor gazing intently through the window, his eyes fixed upon the heavens. It was some time before the Emperor noticed Rapp's presence. Then, suddenly seizing him by the arm, Napoleon exclaimed, "Look there, up there!"

"I see nothing but a few twinkling stars," replied the aide.

"What!" exclaimed Napoleon excitedly. "Is it possible that you do not see my star? The fiery red one, almost as large as the moon? It is before you now, and, ah! how brilliant." Then, warming up at the sight, he fairly shrieked as he cried out, "It has never abandoned me for a single instant. I see it on all great occasions; it commands me to go forward; it is my sign of good fortune, and where it leads I will follow."

In addition to his lucky star of destiny, Napoleon relied on a five-hundred-year-old book on divination and omens, which he consulted prior to most undertakings in order to determine by an elaborate and complicated formula those days that were most likely to be fortuitous.

Napoleon was also a firm believer in presentiments—feelings about events before they happen. Once, after he had become emperor, he was anxiously awaiting news from Egypt, when he heard that one of his Nile boats had run ashore and that the French crew had been put to death. The boat bore the name of *L'Italie*. Napoleon was much concerned when he heard this last piece of news. He looked upon it as an omen that his hopes of annexing Italy to France were to be shattered. Nothing would induce him to believe the contrary. "My presentiments never deceive me," he said, "and all is ruined. I am satisfied that my conquest is lost." In this case the foreboding came true.

Napoleon was not completely free even of ordinary superstitions. He always carried with him a picture of Josephine, his first queen. When the glass over the picture cracked, he is said to have turned pale and declared, "My wife is either sick or unfaithful." (She was unfaithful.)

A talisman Napoleon wore was a scarab he had found in the tomb of an Egyptian king during one of his campaigns. At the climax of his career he gave this charm to the Princess of Schwarzenberg in gratitude for her assistance in arranging his marriage to Marie Louise, the daughter of Emperor Francis I of Austria. He told the princess that he no longer needed the scarab. Nevertheless, his downfall began almost immediately after that, and some have said that he gave his luck away with the scarab.

Statesmen have frequently been the followers of pet superstitions. For example, the first Chancellor of the German Empire, Prince Otto von Bismarck, believed that the number thirteen had great significance for him. He would never sit down at a dinner table when he was the thirteenth person present. His son once recorded that one day after the Franco-Prussian War, when Bismarck gave a dinner at Rheims, one of the invitations had to be canceled at the last moment because otherwise he would have been the thirteenth at the table.

Later in that year, when peace was being negotiated at Versailles, General Boyer, the envoy representing Marshal Bazaine, the commander in chief of the defeated French Army, arrived at the German headquarters on Friday, October 1. Bismarck refused to receive him until the next day, saying that he would never do anything of importance on a Friday, especially negotiate with the French, for it was on a Friday, on October 14, 1806, that during the Napoleonic Wars the French defeated the Prussians twice in one day, in the battles of Jena and Auerstädt. Once, while discussing a day when the Prussians had been defeated by the French earlier in 1870, Bismarck commented "I beg you to observe, gentlemen, that that happened on a Friday."

Several American politicians scrupulously observed their favored superstitions. Thaddeus Stevens, a congressman who was a leader in the Reconstruction following the Civil War, believed that there was luck in picking up pins; he never passed one by if he saw it. James Blaine, secretary of state under three Presidents, would never turn back to enter his house after he had left it, even when he had forgotten something. Secretary of the Treasury Charles Folger, a member of President Chester Arthur's cabinet, firmly believed that the number three was lucky for him and even joked about it. John Carlisle, President Grover Cleveland's secretary of the treasury, would begin no undertaking on a Friday.

As for military men, we have the confession of Lord Wolseley, who became commander in chief of the British Army in 1895. Unlike most prominent persons, he freely admitted that he was superstitious.

> I not only firmly believe in many superstitions [he wrote], but I hug them with the warmest affection. They link me, if not with a spiritual world of which I know nothing, at least with a glorious and artistic and picturesque past of which history has told me much. I believe in ghosts and amulets. I would not, on any account, walk under a ladder. In fact, I am prone to adopt any superstition I am told of which I find others believe in.

General Ulysses Grant became a military man by a lucky chance: He was accepted at the United States Military Academy at West Point when his rival for the appointment from Illinois was found to have six toes on each foot instead of five! Grant was a firm believer in dreams, and he was certain that a dream of dishes was sure to be followed by good luck. The night before he received his appointment as colonel of an Illinois regiment he dreamed of being in a field filled with beautiful china. He immediately woke up his wife and told her that prosperity was about to dawn upon them.

Literary men have not been free from false beliefs.

Shakespeare believed that sleeping in a bed that was more than four hundred years old brought him good luck. James Boswell, in his biography of his companion Dr. Samuel Johnson, noted that his friend and idol never took a walk without touching every lamppost along the way, and that his first step out of doors was always taken with his right foot. Johnson was also very careful lest he walk on the cracks between the paving stones.

Lord Byron, the poet, considered Friday to be an unlucky day. He defied this superstition by setting sail from Italy to Greece on a Friday and died of exposure soon after his arrival, also on a Friday.

Before the fall of the great monarchies after World War I, an observer reported that at least eight of the rulers of European countries had official astrologers, "who were called upon almost daily for prophecies." The last two Russian czars of the Romanov dynasty were extremely superstitious. The reign of Alexander III (1881-1894) was marked by constant revolts and Jewish pogroms, and he lived in fear of being assassinated like his father, Alexander II. He came to depend upon astrologers and sorcerers for advice on his every movement. After his train was wrecked by nihilists, he sent his chief court astrologer, a Tartar, into exile in Siberia because the man had declared that that day was a propitious one for traveling.

His son, Nicholas II, a weak but well-meaning ruler, permitted the evil monk Rasputin to dominate his wife, Empress Alexandra, and finally through her to gain control over him. He was also influenced by an American spiritualist; he would postpone important appointments with representatives of other nations because this adviser had decided that the stars for that day were unfavorable. When one of the most distinguished English diplomats was assigned to the post of ambassador to Russia, he was declared to be unacceptable at the Czar's court because Nicholas had been assured by his astrologer that the diplomat possessed the evil eye.

King Humbert I of Italy (1878-1900) believed that the rare bezoar stone, a glittering calcium growth found in the stomachs or intestines of certain mountain animals, could ward off the evil eye. He wore three such stones in a bracelet, which was welded around his wrist and therefore irremovable. Humbert escaped two attempts on his life, but, in spite of this assumed protection, was finally assassinated.

In the Middle East Muszaffar-ed-Din, the Shah of Persia (1896-1907), whose father had been assassinated, always carried a circle of amber with him when he traveled. This amber was said to have fallen from heaven in Mohammed's time and was believed to render the wearer invulnerable. The Shah also carried a casket, which supposedly made him invisible at will. He credited these talismans with his escape from an assassination attempt in 1900 near Paris while he was on a trip to the French capital. At all times he wore as a necklace a jeweled star that was considered potent in making conspirators against the throne instantly confess to their crimes.

United States President Woodrow Wilson seemed to go to the opposite extreme when he set out to discredit superstition. Wilson was often characterized as a joyless man, burdened by problems and decisions, and lacking a sense of humor. However, he took great delight in having thirteen seated at White House dinners.

Colonel Edward House, Wilson's closest adviser and friend, noted in his diary that when they were preparing the items that were to form the basis of the peace negotiations of World War I, the President laughingly said that he wished the Fourteen Points could be reduced to thirteen. He even suggested that the one on the freedom of the seas, which some of the Allies had strongly objected to in the draft, be eliminated.

At the first dinner of the American delegation to the Versailles Peace Conference, Wilson invited twelve guests and even announced to them that he regarded thirteen as a lucky number. However, when his plan for the League of Nations was not accepted by his own country, he became a bitter man, and some of his enemies pointed out in all seriousness that his downfall was due to his failure to observe the superstition of the unlucky thirteen.

In more recent times, Adolf Hitler, like Napoleon, believed in a star of destiny. In addition, he always consulted a personal soothsayer, who guided him in his actions. Hitler was an absolute dictator and personally made every decision of importance. Yet time after time he refused to give an order until he was able to reach this man, whose name has never been revealed, and to obtain the advice he needed. He inevitably acted upon it immediately. In their autobiographies many of his advisers and associates describe Hitler's insecurity, which was reflected in intense panic when the seer was not present.

Several articles written during the distinguished career of Winston Churchill mention his belief that Friday was an unlucky day and that Friday the thirteenth was even more unfortunate. One author, for example, stated, "Prime Minister Churchill hates Fridays so much that he avoids traveling on them as often as possible, and no mathematician in the world could argue him out of his room if the Friday also happens to be the thirteenth of the month." If this particular idiosyncrasy is true, it might make Churchill seem even more human in the view of many of his admirers. However, no reference is made to his belief in the memoirs of two of those closest to him, his aide and his secretary, although they describe his characteristics in minute detail. Similarly, none of the tributes made to him after his death by people who knew him well included any mention of this belief.

A reasonable explanation might be that an addiction to superstition is often considered a sign of weakness, and most biographers would rather emphasize the virtues of their subjects. That is why current information on the beliefs of world figures and the possible influence of those beliefs on their decisions and actions is almost impossible to discover.

3. Are You Superstitious?

> "Superstition has been defined as the survival of old beliefs in the midst of a new order of things."
> —Charles J. S. Thompson, American anthropologist, *The Hand of Destiny* (1932)

Superstition is alive today, and it is enjoying vigorous and flourishing health. Somewhere in the world at this moment a child may be saying "Cross my heart and hope to die" to assure a playmate that he is speaking the truth. An otherwise rational adult may be knocking on wood— called touching wood by the English—after boasting, making a prediction, or speaking of good fortune. A woman, who has dropped and broken a hand mirror while putting on her makeup, may be shuddering at the thought of the misfortune that will afflict her for the next seven

ARE YOU SUPERSTITIOUS?

years or at the fear that within a year someone in her family will die.

Thousands of people, when waking in the morning, will be sure to climb out of bed on the right side, because if they get up on the left side, the wrong side, everything will go wrong. Before starting the daily routine, they will read their horoscope in the newspaper in order to know what is in store for them and be guided in their actions.

How many people today actually *are* superstitious? To find out, education specialists and psychologists have conducted a number of investigations. They have also sought to determine what type of individual admits to being superstitious, the extent of his acceptance, and the degree to which he lets superstition affect his daily life.

The first (and landmark) study was conducted in 1907 by Professor Fletcher B. Dresslar of the University of California. Dr. Dresslar asked 875 prospective teachers, students in two of California's normal schools, to list all the superstitions they could recall and to indicate their belief or nonbelief in each one. There were 7,100 responses, and the results were:

Expressions of	nonbelief:	52 percent
	partial belief:	30 percent
	total belief:	15 percent
No answer:		3 percent

In other words, about 45 percent of the superstitions recorded were believed to some degree. Dr. Dresslar's conclusion was that "because of the almost universal tendency of the human mind to sparingly acknowledge its own weaknesses and shortcomings, it is safe to say that we have in these results an underestimation, rather than exaggeration, of belief in superstition."

Later studies substantiated the 45 percent figure. A study of 550 students made by Professor Edmund Conklin at the University of Oregon in 1919 revealed that 50 percent admitted belief or practice. At the University of Edinburgh in 1921 Russell Gould, studying Scottish and American students who were enrolled in teacher-training classes, used Dresslar's list. Forty-eight percent of the Scots and 45 percent of the Americans admitted to full belief.

These studies, and later ones, indicate that nearly half the population places faith in superstition. If such investigations included all levels of class and education, the figure might be even higher, perhaps well over a half or as much as three quarters.

Dr. Otis W. Caldwell, for many years the director of the Institute of School Experimentation at Teachers College, Columbia University, made studies of superstitious belief during the 1930's that yielded the most information on the subject. Before his death in 1947 Dr. Caldwell reluctantly admitted to a reporter that, much as he deplored it, his estimates were that 90 percent of the people in the United States were were still influenced to some degree by superstition.

Researchers have agreed that most people develop their interest in superstition during childhood, and learn their first superstitions from older members of their families and from playmates.

In 1933 Julius Maller and Gerhard Lundeen of Dr.

Caldwell's staff studied two groups of pupils, one averaging thirteen years of age, the other sixteen, and questioned them about fifty common superstitions. The pupils mentioned friends as the principal source of their beliefs (27 percent) and the home (23 percent) next. Later studies confirmed these findings.

During the late 1940's Iona and Peter Opie studied five thousand children in England, Scotland, and Wales, and published their findings in 1959 under the title *The Lore and Language of School Children.* In that part of their investigation relating to superstitious belief, the Opies noted that younger children treated the beliefs and rites of their companions more seriously than they did those of their parents and grandparents. However, say the Opies, "it is noticeable that later [from fourteen years old onward] the child-to-child superstitions tend to be discarded along with the rest of the lore, and even forgotten, while the more domestic superstitions, which are passed down in the family, are mentioned with increasing frequency."

When the children were asked how much they believed in their superstitions, most of them said that "all superstitions are silly." Commenting on this, the Opies stated:

> It may be remarked that when a practice or omen is termed a "superstition" it is generally one which is not believed in by the person so referring to it. When collecting this lore from children, we have not asked for "superstitions" as such, but have inquired after the "magic practices" they knew, or asked for their "ways of obtaining luck or averting ill-luck."

Many charms and rites are of course practiced by

children "just for fun," because everybody else practices them, and it is the fashion. Other charms, although recognized as being "probably silly," are repeated because they also feel that there "may be something in it." Others, again, are practiced because it is in the nature of children to be attracted to the mysterious: they appear to have an innate awareness that there is more to the ordering of fate than appears on the surface. And yet other practices and beliefs are undoubtedly so taken for granted that it is not appreciated that the custom or belief is in fact superstitious.

Environment and background also influence superstitious belief. People in rural areas seem to be more tenacious in their faith in it than city dwellers, perhaps because country people live closer to nature and experience its forces at first hand. Many rural superstitions are unique to each locality, while others are variations of popular beliefs. In England the country folk have inherited a body of traditional beliefs and rites of their own. In the United States the people of the southern mountains have an accumulation of singular superstitions that have been handed down from their ancestors. Local remedies for disease, called folk medicine, are the most prevalent.

In Gould's study those who had received their previous education in rural communities recalled a greater number of superstitions and were also affected by them to a larger degree than were students from cities. Of the nine hundred students questioned in Lundeen and Caldwell's 1930 "Study of Unfounded Beliefs Among High School Seniors," those living in rural communities had heard of, believed in, and were influenced by a greater number of superstitions than those in urban areas.

An exception might be found in the ghettos of large cities, where life can be so desperate and ugly that belief in superstition and magic seems to bring a measure of hope to those who are trapped there. Among the American Negroes who live in these ghettos, superstition is one of the major inheritances from Africa. Fortune-tellers and spiritual readers thrive in urban ghettos, and "signs" of success in undertakings, of danger, and of changes in weather, which are common in the rural South, are almost as prevalent among Negroes in the city. Many blacks, particularly those who are natives of Caribbean islands, believe in the evil eye and in the existence of evil spirits, which must be exorcised by the casting of charms and spells.

That girls believe in superstition more than boys, and women more than men, is commonly revealed in studies. In almost every one the number of girls acknowledging belief was 20 to 25 percent more than the number of boys. Conklin's study of 550 college students reported the percentage of women who believed as 60 percent, contrasted with 40 percent of the men. Howard Nixon's study of 350 Columbia University extension students also emphasized the fact that when they were asked to prepare lists of superstitions that they accepted without question, the women submitted a much longer list.

In other investigations, when the subjects were asked what superstitions they formerly believed but did not believe anymore, the women appeared to have clung to their past beliefs more firmly than the men. Conklin found that 90 percent of the women, contrasted with 73 percent of the men, could recall believing in or practicing superstitions at some time in their life. He commented that women were especially inclined to believe in superstitions that concerned wishes, love, marriage, the home, and death.

Investigators who sought to determine a possible relationship between superstition and intelligence reported definitely that none existed. More revealing were the findings related to the education of those tested. Several studies of college students showed that the amount of education an individual possesses apparently does not reduce his belief in superstition.

Astounded by the extent of the beliefs of the 875 California normal-school students questioned in Dresslar's early 1907 study, H. Addington Bruce, of Cambridge, Massachusetts, a contributing editor of *Outlook,* conducted his own informal study among members of the Harvard University faculty—professors, instructors, and assistants who were mostly connected with the departments of history, philosophy, and science. All of them, of course, were educated men who had been "trained in the use of their reasoning powers."

Dr. Bruce used the same questions as Dresslar. After he had completed his inquiry, to his complete surprise—he had anticipated that perhaps 10 or 15 percent of those he questioned would acknowledge some measure of superstitious belief—the Dresslar figures were confirmed. Actually, only 27 percent, after careful deliberation in marking the questionnaire, indicated that they were "absolutely free from superstition," and interestingly enough, they were members of the science faculty. The remaining 73 percent, although in no case admitting "full belief," confessed that in their daily lives they had little habits and customs that indicated they were under superstitious influences, either consciously or unconsciously. "Nor is it without significance," Mr. Bruce commented, "that of this large percentage of true believers, a large proportion at first denied, sometimes with indignation, that they were in the slightest degree superstitious, their denials weakening only after close questioning had led them to look into the matter more carefully."

As Dr. Fletcher Dresslar pointed out in 1907, there is a tendency of the human mind to conceal its weaknesses and shortcomings. Somewhat sheepishly, for example, many individuals will knock on wood to ensure the continuation of their good luck, excusing it with a justification, such as "just in case" or "I know it makes no difference, but maybe ..." Many of the popular superstitions have been so firmly fixed in people's minds that they follow them almost routinely without questioning their efficacy.

The Woman's Home Companion, one of the leading women's magazines in the United States for many years during the first half of the twentieth century, polled two thousand of its readers each month on various questions. Those polled represented a cross section of their 3,700,000 subscribers. The subject of the fifty-eighth poll, in 1947, concerned "pet superstitions." The question read, "Have you a pet superstition? If yes, what is it?" Seven out of ten of the respondents admitted they had favorite beliefs, and altogether more than two hundred were named. (Nine of the thirteen reported most often are listed in the quiz in this chapter.)

The respondents often added comments, confessing that they were ashamed to admit their allegiance to certain beliefs. "I know it's foolish, but I feel a little safer if I knock on wood after boasting," said one. Another, who insisted that she had no superstitions at all, added a footnote to the form: "I didn't think I had a pet superstition, but last night I walked around my chair to change my luck at bridge and got a hand on which I bid and made a grand slam! So please change my vote from 'No' to 'Yes.'"

A list of the most commonly accepted superstitions is not difficult to compile. The specific superstitions selected in the quiz that follows represent those recorded as "most-believed" by the largest number of people. The participants in these studies were high-school, college, and university students.

How Superstitious Are You?

Twenty-five of the most popular superstitions are listed below. Do you believe in them? Score yourself five for every Yes answer and zero for every No. If the total is over one hundred, you may consider yourself to be very superstitious; if it is between fifty and a hundred, you are normally superstitious; and if it is below fifty, you may pride yourself on being less superstitious than the average person.

ARE YOU SUPERSTITIOUS?

1. If you first look at the new moon over the right shoulder, your luck will be good for the next month; if over the left, misfortune will follow.
2. Finding a pin with the point lying toward you means good luck; head toward you means bad luck.
3. Wearing or carrying charms, lucky pieces, or amulets brings good luck.
4. Carrying a rabbit's foot brings good luck.
5. Finding a four-leaf clover brings good luck, as does carrying it.
6. A horseshoe brings good luck.
7. A horseshoe over a door with the open end up brings good fortune to the house.
8. Seven is a lucky number.
9. Three is lucky.
10. On his birthday a person should receive a slap on the back for each year he has lived and an extra one for good luck in the next year.
11. It is unlucky to have anything to do with the number thirteen.
12. There should never be thirteen seated at a dinner table.
13. Friday the thirteenth is an unlucky day, and one should be unusually cautious on that day; beginning an undertaking or starting a new task then dooms it to certain failure.
14. Walking under a ladder will bring bad luck.
15. Opening an umbrella in a house is sure to bring bad luck.
16. Breaking a mirror brings misfortune ("for seven years" is often added) or foretells tragedy soon to come.
17. When a black cat crosses your path, bad luck is sure to follow.

18. Lighting three cigarettes with one match brings bad luck.
19. If you spill salt at the table, you must throw a little over your left shoulder to prevent bad luck or a quarrel with a friend. (The death of one of those at the table may also be anticipated.)
20. Always get in and out of bed on the right side; you will become cross and irritable when you get up on the wrong (left) side.
21. When someone sneezes, you should say something like "God bless you!" or "Gesundheit!" to avert bad luck.
22. If you boast about your good luck, knock on wood ("three times" is sometimes added) to keep your luck from changing.
23. If you make a wish on seeing the first star in the evening, your wish will come true. This is usually accompanied by the following folk rhyme:

> Starlight, star bright,
> First star I see tonight;
> Wish I may, wish I might,
> Have the wish I wish tonight.

24. You should make a wish on seeing a falling star.
25. The person who gets the largest part when pulling a wishbone will see the fulfillment of the wish he has made (he must not tell what his wish is).

If, after you have totaled your score, you want to compare your Yes answers with those who answered positively in the studies, you will find a list of them at the end of the book on page 190.

4. Unfounded Beliefs

> "A foolish superstition introduces the influences of the gods even in the smallest matters."
> —Livy, Roman historian, *History of Rome* (A.D. 10)

All superstitions are, of course, false beliefs. A large body of them, however, are beliefs that were once accepted as true, but which have since been disproved by scientific evidence. Almost everyone at some time or other quotes one of these false sayings as if it were authentic, and as a result belief in them is still strong. The following are among the most prevalent:

Body Features

A person's character can be read by noting the shape of his head or its unusual features.

Phrenologists maintain that certain mental faculties and character traits are indicated by the shape and configuration of one's skull. Scientists disagree completely.

A high forehead indicates intellectual superiority.

Slightly different from the belief of phrenologists, this statement is associated with the erroneous notion that the larger the head is, the larger the brain is. Anthropologists say there is no difference intellectually between the "highbrow" and the "lowbrow."

A square jaw is a sign of willpower, a receding chin a sign of weak character.

The assumption of this belief is that mental qualities are expressed by physical characteristics. Determination to perform a difficult task may often be accompanied by clenched teeth and a set jaw, thus suggesting an association between the shape of a person's jawbone and his willpower. Similarly, the fallacy of the receding jaw is another misconceived notion concerning the supposed ease with which we can tell a person's intelligence from his facial expression.

Long, slender hands indicate an artistic nature.

Palmists and fortune-tellers say that the shape of the hand reveals mental and vocational abilities, and they agree that long, slender hands show an artistic nature. Physiologists, however, disagree. Just as many artists have short fingers as have long, tapering ones. Sculptors and pianists may find the latter valuable, but the generalization does not apply.

Male-Female Differences

Women are inferior to men in intelligence.

Men who are questioned profess this belief more frequently than women. However, intelligence has nothing to do with sex.

Men are superior to women because they are more rational in their thinking.

This unfounded belief is based on the assumption that women are more subjective and emotional than men, just as men are supposed to be more objective. The Women's Liberation movement is attempting to alter this image.

Women possess a power of intuition absent in men.

Intuition—quick and ready insight—is not limited to women. The erroneous belief is probably related to the belief that women are inclined to be more emotional and subjective than men.

Women are by nature purer and nobler than men.

This generalization is without any foundation whatsoever and is based on the long-prevailing idea of the female who is protected from the world of reality. In the contemporary world women are rarely so protected, and any difference between men and women depends on environment and training.

Misconceptions About Negroes

In an article published by *Newsweek* in 1963, when the civil rights movement was just beginning, William Brink and Louis Harris discussed the results of a poll among whites, both nationwide and in the South, which revealed many of their stereotyped beliefs regarding Negroes.* The

---

*Newsweek, Vol. 62 (July 29, 1963), pp. 15-36. Expanded in book form by William J. Brink and Louis Harris, *The Negro Revolution in America*. New York, Simon and Schuster, 1964.

study also sought to discover whether prejudice diminished when whites had social contact with blacks.

The respondents were given a series of ten popular beliefs and then asked which statements they agreed with and which they rejected. The results:

		Percentage who agree with statement		Those with previous social contact with blacks
	Nationwide	South		
Negroes laugh a lot.	68	81		79
Negroes tend to have less ambition.	66	81		56
Negroes smell different.	60	78		50
Negroes have looser morals.	55	80		39
Negroes keep untidy homes.	46	57		31
Negroes want to live off the handout.	41	61		26
Negroes have less native intelligence.	39	60		23
Negroes breed crime.	35	46		21
Negroes are inferior to whites.	31	51		15
Negroes care less for the family.	31	49		22

Notice particularly the lower percentages for those who have had contact with blacks.

A few implanted beliefs about Negroes are worthy of comment:

Negroes are like children.

This belief is based on the assumption that all "primitive" people are childlike and naturally happy, and that, since present-day blacks are descendants of Africans, they are close to the primitive state. In the United States this misconception arose during the years of slavery, when plantation owners and overseers, having stripped Negroes of even the most basic human rights, looked upon them as children.

Negroes are naturally happy and carefree.

This unfounded belief also stems from the time when blacks were slaves and when their few pleasures derived from socialization among themselves, which was accompanied by laughter.

Negroes are "shiftless," lack moral standards, and care less for the family.

The conviction that blacks lack ambition comes from the fact that over the years American society has offered them meager opportunity for advancement. Conditions in the black city ghettos breed crime, and there is a high incidence of broken and fatherless families. Poor economic conditions and welfare laws that encourage fathers to leave home result in a matriarchal society. There is no indication, however, that blacks "care less" for their families than whites.

Blacks are not as intelligent as whites.

When University of California psychologist Arthur Jensen declared in 1969 that in some forms of intelligence the Negro is genetically doomed to a lower position than the white, he provoked an academic storm that has yet to subside. Professor Franklin Hall of Johns Hopkins University investigated an assortment of brains of various ethnic origins and concluded that the brains of whites cannot be distinguished from those of Negroes. As to intelligence itself, in 1971 Irwin Katz, a psychologist at

New York University, reported that blacks rated fifteen to twenty points below whites when the test they were taking was identified as an IQ (intelligence quotient) test, but they were equal to whites when told it was an experiment to help plan the curriculum. West Indians in an English secondary school were tested the same way, with identical results. The conclusion was that black students were thoroughly aware of the judgment of inferiority held by many whites, and accordingly fell behind when they felt both challenged and anxious.

Negroes smell different.

That blacks have an odor characteristic of their race, while not completely untrue, is based on the implied assumption that this condition is unique to Negroes. A person's odor depends on what he eats and wears and on his habits of personal health and cleanliness. A person's body odor also reflects his environment. In two American studies no differences could be detected between whites and blacks, given similar conditions of diet and cleanliness, so this belief must be attributed to ingrown prejudice. As a matter of fact, blacks insist that whites have a definite odor!

Infants and Children

By fixing her mind on a subject, an expectant mother can influence the character of her unborn child.

This erroneous belief, which flourished especially during the Victorian period, held particularly that a pregnant woman should visit art galleries or attend concerts so that her child might be "artistically inclined."

If a pregnant woman is frightened, her child will probably bear a birthmark.

The persistence of this fallacy is undoubtedly due to its appearance in literature. A birthmark is due to a blood-vessel split, and gynecologists affirm with certainty that there is no connection between the mother's nervous system and her unborn child. The stories are therefore mere coincidences.

A child comes into the world with an instinctive knowledge of good and evil. This is his conscience, and it is born in him.

Concepts of right and wrong are influenced by parents, the school, and the church. They are inculcated.

Particularly intelligent children are likely to be physically weak.

Professor Lewis Terman of Stanford University studied the life histories of a thousand brilliant children, many of them true prodigies, through ten years of their growth. He found that not only were they somewhat healthier and stronger than average children, but not a single one showed any tendency toward weakness or ill health.

If a child is good-looking, he will grow up to be ugly; if ugly, he will become good-looking.

Anyone who observes the physical development of children into adulthood knows this belief to be untrue. The beautiful baby is apt to be good-looking all his life.

Miscellaneous Beliefs

Fear or an emotional shock can cause the hair to turn gray or white overnight.

Though numerous stories are told of this phenomenon,

none has been scientifically authenticated. Instances of it are cited abundantly in both literature (Byron's *The Prisoner of Chillon* and several of the horror stories of Edgar Allan Poe, for example) and history. Marie Antoinette and Mary Queen of Scots were said to have had their hair turn white on their way to the scaffold. King Henry IV, "troubled by the prospect of war," we are told, "put his head in his hands to meditate on his sorrows," and, when he looked up, his moustache had turned white! A number of explanations have been advanced. For example, a specialist in the field has stated that "shock, rage, and fear cause the appearance in the skin of the scalp of tiny bubbles whose refraction gives the hair its whiteness," but other specialists deny that this is possible. Finally, the *Journal of the American Medical Association* concluded editorially in 1948 that "reports of sudden blanching of the hair must be regarded as inherently improbable."

Fish is a brain food.

Nutritional scientists state that no food has more value, as far as the brain is concerned, than any other. The extraordinary development of the brain in infants occurs during the time of life when the chief item in their diet is milk. Calcium, however, is recognized as being valuable in bone development.

Appendicitis may be caused by swallowing seeds.

This false belief is widely held by children. Most people who eat grapes, watermelon, and oranges swallow some seeds at one time or another. Yet appendicitis practically never results; surgeons rarely find a seed, and even then it is not the seed that is the cause of the inflammation, but pus-forming germs.

5. A Little Bit of Luck

> "Look, how the world's poor people are amazed
> At apparitions, signs and prodigies!"
> —William Shakespeare, *Venus and Adonis* (1593)

It would be impossible to guess the number of people who feel that the element of luck influences their lives. However, the information supplied by researchers does give a clue. When, in Caldwell and Lundeen's landmark study, nine hundred American respondents were asked the question "Do you think of yourself as a lucky person?" 30 percent gave a positive response. In Scotland 43 percent of the 265 persons in a Glasglow inquiry acknowledged that they believed in luck; 23 percent felt they were born lucky; 20 percent felt they were born unlucky. A

German study, involving a thousand respondents, requested answers to the question "Do you find that you have in your life runs of good and bad luck, or have you not noticed anything like that?" Fifty-four percent answered that they had experienced both.

Such evidence indicates that belief in good and bad luck still plays an important part in contemporary life.

A large part of superstition, perhaps as much as a third of it, concerns luck. For instance, practically everybody apparently believes that finding a four-leaf clover means good luck, and most of us have spent time searching for them in scattered clover patches. A traditional saying explains the lucky powers associated with the four-leaf clover:

> One leaf for fame, one leaf for wealth,
> And one leaf for a faithful lover,
> And one leaf to bring glorious health—
> All are in a four-leaf clover.

The reason for the four-leaf clover's popularity is lost in antiquity, but there is a legend that Eve, when she was expelled from paradise, took a four-leaf clover with her, thus giving it a reputation for good luck. The saying "He's in clover" means "He's enjoying good luck." In Ireland the four-leafed shamrock is the equivalent of the four-leaf clover. Incidentally, if you ever find an extremely rare five-leaf clover, it is supposed to be a sign that money is coming to you.

City dwellers can now buy four-leaf clovers sealed in plastic and on chains or key rings. In fact, the cultivation

A LITTLE BIT OF LUCK

of commercial four-leaf clovers has become a profitable business.

The rabbit's foot is the clover's chief rival. The rabbit is a prolific animal, producing large numbers of offspring. For that reason it was thought to possess a creative power superior to other animals, and thus became associated with prosperity and success. If a person carries a rabbit's foot, preferably the left hind foot, good luck is sure to follow. True believers stroke their hands or faces with it, so they will have success in a new venture. Primitive tribes often used the feet of small animals as charms, but why the foot should be associated with good fortune has never been satisfactorily explained.

For many years the late Charles Brand, a New York furrier, was the chief commercial source of rabbits' feet in the United States. Through the years his firm produced twenty million rabbit paws for watch fobs and key chains. Before 1938, when Mr. Brand decided to make it his occupation, only a jeweler could cap a foot so that it could be worn on a chain. Mr. Brand developed a die that could turn out fifty thousand a day. He obtained the feet in bale lots from California and from rabbit hunters throughout the country. Cut to size, mothproofed, sterilized, cleaned, and then capped and chained, the finished paw was sold to novelty shops. Current production is not recorded, but the demand is continuous.

One good-luck superstition that is almost uniquely English, though it is practiced to a lesser extent in Austria and Germany, is "sweep's luck." Where and how the idea originated is not precisely known, although superstitions involving sweeping and brooms are numerous. George L. Phillips, writing in the *American Journal of Folklore*, recounts an "improbable legend" as to the origin of the sweep's-luck superstition in England. An alert chimney sweep is said to have caught the reins of a frightened horse running away with one of the early Georges, probably during the eighteenth century. As a mark of gratitude, the rescued king doffed his hat and bowed to sweepdom in general. He could not recognize his benefactor because of the soot and dirt on his face. The king's courtiers and then the common people followed His Majesty's example, and in the course of years the practice became a habit. Thus arose the belief that all sweeps were lucky fellows.

An Englishman, meeting a chimney sweep who is making his rounds the first thing in the morning, feels that the day will be a lucky one. Racing fans will often refuse to place bets on the horses unless they have seen a sweep earlier in the day. Some Britishers believe the sweep should be touched. The clasp of his dirty hand, the friendly wave of his arm, or his smile are still considered to be certain evidence of his blessing.

The presence of a sweep at British weddings is particularly desirable and is as much of a tradition as "something old, something new, something borrowed, something blue" and the throwing of rice. "It is a brave bride in Britain," writes an observer, "who will risk taking off on her honeymoon without a kiss—a peck on the cheek is sufficient—from a sooty sweep for good luck. Some of the finicky ones will settle for a handshake, which the groom always receives, and even the most aloof bride agrees that for a wedding to be a success, a chimney sweep should at least be on hand." The custom is observed by both the high and the low in the social structure. When Prince Philip married the then Princess Elizabeth in 1947, he left his apartment in Buckingham Palace before the royal procession departed and shook the dirty hand of a sweep who "chanced" to be loitering at the entrance to the royal residence.

In warm weather English sweeps deliberately stand outside fashionable churches where weddings are scheduled. When the bride trips down the steps, they offer to kiss her cheek and shake the groom's hand as a blessing to the married couple, and the newspapers invariably mention the action. Money is of course given to them.

Sweep's luck is not as much sought after today as in the past, but the tradition has far from disappeared from the English scene.

Superstitions about bad luck abound also. In fact, they are seemingly endless. Here are just a few of the most popular ones:

It is bad luck to watch a person out of sight, for if you watch him, you will never see him again.

You should not turn back for something you have forgotten after starting on a journey, or you will have bad luck.

You should take off the left shoe first when undressing, because taking the right one off first means bad luck. You should put on your left shoe first to avoid bad luck. It is bad luck to put your shoes on a table.

It is bad luck to change a garment that you have accidentally put on wrong side out.

Breaking a dish is a sign of coming bad luck.

Taking a broom along when moving to another house brings bad luck.

Removing a ring from the finger of a friend brings bad luck to him. It is bad luck to remove a wedding ring from the owner's finger.

Wearing opals brings bad luck, because they are very unlucky.

To kill a spider brings bad luck.

When walking with a friend, you should never let an object like a post come between you; if it does, say "bread and butter" to avert bad luck or a quarrel.

If two persons wipe their hands at the same time, it means a quarrel, but they can avoid it by twisting the towel.

If you stumble on the street curb or over any other object, go back and walk over it properly to avert bad luck.

If you shake hands twice in saying good-bye, do it a third time to avoid bad luck.

You should leave a house by the same door you used in entering it to avoid misfortune.

If you give a knife to a friend as a gift, he must give you a present or a penny, or it will cut (end) your friendship.

The four most frequently recognized and practiced bad-luck superstitions are the black cat, breaking a mirror, the number thirteen, and walking under a ladder.

An interesting experiment involving a ladder was conducted in 1960 by members of a psychology class at Bishop Otter College in Chichester, England. The purpose

A LITTLE BIT OF LUCK

of the experiment was to observe the reactions of pedestrians when confronted by two ladders on a busy street in Sheffield. Each ladder was placed so that it was easy to pass under it and dangerous to walk around it, because to do so one had to step out into the heavy traffic.

The first ladder was in position for only two minutes. During that time a window cleaner was working on it. Of thirty-five pedestrians, six (three men and three women) passed under the ladder. Twenty-nine people took the dangerous course of stepping into the road rather than going under it.

Since it might be said that most of the pedestrians stepped off the sidewalk to avoid the first ladder because the worker might drop something on them, the second ladder was left empty. It remained in position on a street with less traffic for fifteen minutes. Out of fifty-two pedestrians, fourteen passed under the ladder (six women and eight men), and thirty-eight stepped into the road to avoid it.

This experiment offered abundant evidence that belief in the ladder superstition is still strong today.

A phase of bad luck that particularly worries the superstitious is the jinx—a person, thing, or influence supposed to bring continual ill luck to an individual. It is referred to as "a run of back luck." The jinx is a hazard to the professional gambler, and actors consider themselves to be jinxed when several successive productions have short runs or are failures. Accident-prone individuals are said to be jinxed.

When a series of misfortunes occurs, it is often the

result of the person's fatalistic attitude, because he feels that he is basically unlucky and therefore does nothing to avoid having things happen to him. The bad luck may continue until the cause is discovered and removed.

A jinx may exist over a long period of time, but the person affected must wait until "his luck changes," because bad luck is believed to occur in more than a single incident or event. This is attested to in two very popular superstitions: "Misfortunes never come singly" and "One disappointment is followed by two others." In the United States the latter is also expressed as "Bad things happen in threes." This saying applies particularly to the deaths of prominent individuals. When a well-known actor, director, or producer dies in Hollywood, the members of the motion-picture industry await with trepidation the announcement of two additional deaths. By an odd coincidence, that is what often happens. The three-on-a-match superstition is another example. The belief in three as an unlucky number supposedly arose from the fact that Peter denied Jesus three times "before the cock crows."

In spite of the above, three is also considered to be a very lucky number, because it has always been a figure of mystical significance and power. Birth needed three people—father, mother, and child—so three came to mean life itself. Three is frequently a symbolic number in religion. The Holy Trinity is expressed as the Father, Son, and Holy Ghost. Pagans saw three in the earth, sea, and sky.

Superstitions regarding lucky and unlucky numbers are universally believed, particularly about the lucky seven

A LITTLE BIT OF LUCK

and the unlucky thirteen. The latter is without doubt the most heeded of all superstitions. Many of the most modern hotels, apartment houses, and office buildings in large cities omit the thirteenth floor and have no room numbers containing thirteen. Some airlines refuse to have a Flight 13 or even seats with that number. In Paris, only a few houses bear the number thirteen; they are likely to skip from twelve to fourteen, or sometimes what would ordinarily be numbered thirteen is "twelve *bis*" ("twelve twice"). Many of those who usually scoff at superstitious belief had second thoughts during the flight of Apollo 13, which was launched on April 11, 1970. Two days later, *on the thirteenth,* the explosion of an oxygen tank canceled the moon mission and placed the lives of the three astronauts in desperate danger. The whole world seemed to hold its breath as the crew used the landing module as a lifeboat to sustain them during the long, arduous trip back to earth with a "dead" space capsule.

Not only numbers, but days as well are thought to be both lucky and unlucky. Sunday is generally lucky, though so-called "blue laws" must be scrupulously observed. Monday is generally lucky, except in Russia and Germany. Tuesday is free from ill luck, but Wednesday, because some people believe it was the day Judas betrayed Jesus, should be watched with care. Thursday is very unlucky, a day of judgment and crises, when anything can happen. Friday, of course, is generally thought to be unlucky, but when it occurs on the thirteenth, disaster is likely to result. Saturday can be either good or bad. The answer to how these beliefs developed lies in the distant past.

One of the oldest British superstitions for avoiding bad luck concerns seeing a white horse. The belief appears in many versions, the most quoted being "On seeing a white horse, you should spit and make a wish." Spittle, like blood, was once thought to be a source of power and therefore a potent agent of magic, to be used for protection and success. According to Pliny, the Roman naturalist, the act of spitting protected against witches and was a charm against evil. Today expectorating on a coin is thought to assure good fortune; boxers spit on their hands before a bout, and dice players often spit on the cubes before a throw.

Wishes and luck have always been related. Very early in their lives children begin to make wishes and often accompany them with acts or rituals and traditional rhymes. The most accepted wish superstition concerns seeing the first star or a falling star. Blowing out the candles on a birthday cake is another. This action is assumed to bring good fortune to the celebrant for the coming year. The custom originated with the Greeks, for whom a candle symbolized life. The number of candles on the cake should be the number of years of life already attained. Successfully blowing them out in one breath after making a wish will make the wish come true. On the other hand, if you tell your wish, it will not come true.

Wishes are not always made to obtain positive results. Curses have been used to bring ill luck to others in both primitive and modern societies. Casting a spell is the same as uttering a curse. For example, in voodooism, which comes from the Caribbean and originally Africa, the person to be cursed is supposed to suffer from the incantations and rituals directed toward an object or doll that represents him. Italians, particularly Neapolitans and Sicilians, often believe in the power of ill-wishing curses, and in the ghettos of large American cities bad-luck tokens and books of charms and spells, to be used in causing ill luck or harm to others, are bought and sold.

Luck, fickle fortune, and chance form the basis for all gambling, or gaming. As a result, everyone who bets, wagers, speculates, throws dice, or plays for stakes is innately superstitious. In fact, the reliance that serious gamblers place upon luck is so unwavering that, as a group, they are the slaves of superstition.
The gambling impulse is as old as history. Gamblers practiced their skills in ancient Egypt. In the European countries, particularly among the wealthy and titled in France and England, it became almost a madness. Today all who indulge in it worship Lady Luck and the hazards of chance. Even the ordinary cardplayer, who plays for low stakes or none at all, assumes that a lucky turn of the cards may make him a winner.
Compulsive gamblers have always existed, both as professionals and amateurs, but their number has increased phenomenally in modern times, and such gambling is now recognized as an illness. The principal aim of the neurotic gambler is not to gain money; he seldom if ever quits when he has made a "killing." He continues to gamble until he loses again. Instead of discouraging or disheartening him, bad luck becomes a challenge to be overcome. If his specialty is racetrack betting, he will feverishly anticipate a change of fortune, and has been known to resort to

embezzlement of his employer's funds and the sacrifice of his family's security because of his belief in luck.

Most people lack the dedicated gambler's intense faith in luck, whether good or bad, but the popularity of official lotteries and legalized off-track betting attests to the widespread existence of the gambling instinct.

The custom of tossing a coin in the air to settle a problem or reach a solution—"Heads you win, tails you lose"—is, according to the author Claudia de Lys, "especially popular with those who believe in 'luck.' ... Many of this superstitious type have their own 'lucky' coin, one that they never use in their games, if they are gamblers, for fear of losing it and, with it, the good luck attached to it."

All who gamble invariably carry objects that are intended to bring them success. These vary from the frequent rabbit's foot to the horseshoe, which was used mainly in the past.

The gambler experiences many moods. However, if he is winning by using certain methods, he will continue to use them. This is called "backing one's luck." If the ordinary player has a losing streak, he will quit a game; the compulsive gambler will continue in the desperate hope that his luck will change.

Touching a hunchback brings good luck; the word "hunch" comes from this superstition. Francis Bacon, the English philosopher, wrote, "Deformed persons are commonly evil by nature, for as nature has done ill by them, so they by nature are beings devoid of natural affection." Such believers considered that the hunchback, himself an evil object, could aid in warding off the unseen forces of evil. Traditionally, kings had a hunchback as court jester, not only to amuse the court but also to bring good fortune, because touching the hump could even change bad luck to good. Contemporary Italians still regard this action as a powerful luck bringer.

Hunchbacks often make their living by loitering near European gambling casinos, where they are rewarded for their availability. An internationally known hunchback in Monte Carlo almost became a landmark. He was able to "retire" at an early age in considerable affluence.

Gamblers claim that dice is the most popular game in the United States. It is certainly one of the most ancient games. In the early days either pebbles or knucklebones served as dice, and people believed that the way they fell revealed the will of the gods.

Another name for dice in the United States is "crap shooting." This term originated in France, where young boys who wanted to shoot dice but whose parents objected would stoop like toads in doorways to play. So dice playing was given the name *crapaud,* the French word for toad, which in America has been shortened to "crap." Other names are "bones," "ivories," "galloping dominoes," and "African golf" because of the predilection of blacks for the activity.

The throw of the dice has always been of key importance. Many players talk to the cubes. Such "sweet-talk" appeals as "Baby needs a new pair of shoes" are common. "Come seven, come eleven" is a favorite cry, and snapping the fingers is intended to keep bad luck away and prevent the rolling of "snake eyes," the lowest and losing number. The lucky seven is, of course, most desired. Crapshooters also blow on the dice for luck, or rub them on a red-haired person or their own bodies.

According to Claudia de Lys, many ancient superstitions related to dice and the predicting of fortunes are still believed: Rub the dice on a redheaded person, and it will bring good luck. Carry a pair with you, and you will always have money. If you find a cube with one spot up, you will receive a letter of great importance. If the dice has two spots up, you will take a long and successful trip. Three spots up means that a big surprise awaits you, and you will sleep in a strange bed. Four spots up is very unlucky, for trouble is sure to follow. Five spots up brings unfaithfulness in love or change in family affairs. The six spot is lucky, for it will bring unexpected money.

Of all mass gambling, betting on race horses is the most popular throughout the world. The dedicated player places implicit faith in tips and hunches, meticulously studying the track records of horses in an attempt to determine a possible winning horse on which to place his bet, whether small or large. The "sport of kings," so called because only the wealthy could afford the financial risks involved, is full of superstitions for gamblers.

Most horseplayers believe that they will be lucky if, on a racing day, they accidentally meet a cross-eyed man. Of course, many of them claim to study the odds scientifically, but winning still basically involves chance. For example, a "hunch player" places his bets strictly on the basis of seemingly unimportant or insignificant things that occur just before a race begins. In selecting a winner, the horse bettor often plays these hunches, which may be inspired by the color worn by a jockey or his number in the gate lineup. Confronted with a large number of entries, the bettor may stick a pin at random on the names of horses, some of which may particularly attract him for some personal reason. A confirmed bettor will be undaunted by losses, always hoping that the next race will bring him luck. Indeed, this type of gambling appears to yield more excitement for the bettor than any other.

In the United States the two-dollar bill, withdrawn from circulation in 1966, was considered unlucky, in spite of the fact that the number two is considered to be lucky. In the nineteenth century politicians and political bosses used this bill to pay for votes, and a man with a "deuce" (the old English word for devil) was suspected of having sold his vote.

But the chief source of the superstition was the racetrack. Two dollars was and still is the minimum wager on a horse, and is the bet that is most often made. The two-dollar bill was much favored by the managements because making change with it was easier and faster. But a bettor generally loses more often than he wins, and the jinx belief came about when bettors making two-dollar wagers lost more often than they won. Even nonbettors considered the two-dollar bill unlucky, and some of them believed that the bad luck could be broken by tearing off one corner of the bill. The Treasurer of the United States once stated that over a third of the bills returned were torn and had to be destroyed.

In the fall of 1971 a bill providing for the reissuance of the two-dollar bill was introduced in the House of Representatives. Cashiers at racetracks would welcome the new bill, but they probably hope that its past reputation will not be revived.

Card games, one of the most prominent social activities, can be played for amusement only, and often are. Skilled players, however, play for money, which apparently gives more purpose to the game.

The first modern playing cards were devised in 1392 for the French king Charles VI (1380-1422) to entertain him when he began to have frequent fits of insanity—hence his appellation Charles the Mad. Each of the four suits represented the four classes of French society at that time. Hearts personified the powerful clergy, who were supposed to be kind and just ("to have heart"). The military class was symbolized by the points of spears, which came to be called spades in Britain. The club was related to the clover leaf, the emblem of farmers and peasants. The diamond was chosen to represent the middle class, particularly merchants, who hoarded diamonds as the basis of their wealth. After a while certain powers began to be attached to the card suits, and from these powers grew many of the superstitions related to fortune-telling, or "reading the cards," which is called cartomancy.

The ordinary cardplayer, however, is more interested in the game and in his own good or bad luck. There are many card-playing superstitions. "Unlucky in cards, lucky in love" and its opposite, "Lucky at cards, unlucky in love," are the most quoted sayings, perhaps because the path of love between two persons is considered just as unpredictable as the cards that are dealt in a game of chance.

Serious bridge players often believe that an unlucky player can change his luck by walking around the table or chair—some believe three times—or by asking for a new pack of cards. Poker players are generally serious; from them came the description "poker face," used for someone whose lack of expression offers no clue about the cards he is holding.

Some players kiss the pack of cards for luck before dealing. Playing on a bare table is unlucky, hence the use of the green felt cover in casinos. It is unlucky to lend or borrow money during a game. Sticking a pin in the lapel of a fellow player's coat will bring good luck. The dropping of any card on the floor is a bad omen, and if it is a black ace, the player should quit the game. Singing or humming while a game is in progress dooms the player to losing.

No dogs should be in the room where a poker game is being played, and the cards should not be picked up until the entire hand has been dealt. Looking over someone's shoulder or placing a foot on his chair brings bad luck. Some people believe that cutting the cards will cut off their luck. Good luck is ensured if the player stacks his chips in a neat pile.

There is a common superstition among male cardplayers that it is unlucky to gamble when a woman is present, no matter what game is being played, unless she is a player. This belief is a modern reflection of the fact that, among primitive societies and almost until the eighteenth century, women were excluded from the social activities of men.

Belief in one's luck is probably stronger among gamblers than anyone else. Because of the nature of the game, they can hardly be expected to accept Ralph Waldo Emerson's statement that "shallow men believe in luck."

6. Sports and Superstition

> "Superstition is the poison of the mind."
> —Joseph Lewis, president, Freethinkers of America (1958)

Success or failure in an athletic contest depends mainly on the skill of the opponents. Under such conditions one might reasonably assume that chance or luck would play a relatively minor role in sports, but that is not the case. Athletes in all fields, like gamblers, have their special superstitions. They are notorious in their attachment to good-luck talismans, and few fail to impute power and success to them. The talisman may be a piece of clothing, a charm, or some other item that has, in the athlete's opinion, continually brought success.

In an article on the psychology of sports written in 1930, J. B. M. Clark described the attitude of the athlete.

The workings of the mind in the realm of sport sometimes bring about curious results [he wrote], and a right psychological attitude is often half the battle. If an individual player gets imbued with the notion that he can always beat a certain other player, the idea will go a long way toward helping him do it. It is the same way with teams. A right frame of mind is essential.

The response of fans can affect the delicate psychology of an athlete. Cheers act as an encouragement to him, but booing can shake his confidence. That is one reason why each sport has its own superstitions, to which the players tenaciously cling, and why individuals cherish their own private beliefs as to success or failure.

Baseball is considered America's national sport, and baseball players undoubtedly lead all other athletes in their devotion to superstition. As a class they are probably more susceptible to jinxes than any other body of professional players in the world. Christopher (Christy) Mathewson, pitcher for the New York Giants in the early years of the twentieth century, called baseball "the child of superstition." In his book *Pitching in the Pinch,* written after his retirement, he said, "A jinx can make a bad pitcher out of a good one and a blind batter out of a three hundred hitter."

Luck, he continued, is a combination of confidence and getting the breaks. Ballplayers get no breaks without confidence in themselves. Lucky omens inspire this confidence, and unlucky signs take it away. Once sports reporters and fans begin to label a player "a man who cannot win," the player's confidence in his abilities begins to falter, often with disastrous results. Once acquired, this reputation pursues him, and he quickly goes into a "slump," often never to recover. With their expectations of good performance, baseball fans are cruelly intolerant of an idol who falls from their favor. Without confidence the best player is nothing; with it, according to Mathewson, he can work miracles.

Because of the topsy-turvy nature of the game and the notorious changes in the loyalty of the fans, the players adopt many widely believed superstitions, some seemingly foolish to the average person.

Nearly everyone in baseball is a slave to precedent. If a player has a run of luck one day, he tries to do everything the same the next day, to keep good fortune on his side.

One of the most persistent superstitions of the game is that if a player sees a cross-eyed woman in the stands, he can be hexed, so that he will not get a hit during the game. On the other hand, redheaded women are reputed to be enormously lucky for a ballplayer. If he can take a hairpin from her hair, he is sure to make home runs. Hairpins in general are considered lucky because they mean base hits. When playing with the Dodgers, Leo Durocher collected hairpins of all kinds, and when he was on the road, he continually walked down hotel corridors hunting for more.

Successful big-league fielders often use the same gloves they had when they were on lesser teams, because they think the gloves are lucky. Others are extremely careful about the way they leave their gloves on the ground when they go to bat. They agree that the fingers should always point to their own team's dugout. Among old-time ballplayers it was considered good luck to spit in one's glove. Teams usually consider a "southpaw" (left-handed) pitcher to be good luck.

There are loads of superstitions about bats. Each bat is believed to contain just so many singles, doubles, triples, and home runs. As a result, few players would think of loaning good luck to a teammate. It is also considered very dangerous to permit bats to lie crosswise in front of a dugout. If a bat has a split in it, even a minor one, it should never be used, for it brings bad luck. A bat should never be changed after strike two.

The selection of a bat boy, or mascot, is made very carefully. A black boy was always chosen in the early days of the game, and players habitually rubbed his head before going to bat. The popularity of the Negro mascot declined after a game between the St. Louis Cardinals and the New York Yankees. In a crucial inning, with the bases loaded, the great Babe Ruth was called to bat. Before picking up the bat, he rubbed his hands thoroughly on the kinky hair of the little black boy, who had just been hired to bring luck to the Yanks. Wreathed in smiles and supremely self-confident, Ruth walked to the plate—and struck out. The unfortunate boy was dismissed.

Those who followed the superstition often did the same with a Negro bellboy or shoe-shine boy in a hotel. A hunchback is regarded by ballplayers as the best luck in the world; if a man can just touch the hump before going to the plate, he is sure to get a hit.

For several seasons in the 1920's the Phillies carried a hunchbacked boy with them on all their trips, and voted him a half share of the prize money after winning one world's series. They claimed he won two world's series for them.

As for bad luck, a dog crossing the playing field before the first pitch is sure to bring disaster to the team at bat. It is also bad luck for a team when the first man at bat fans out. On the other hand, the team that loses the first innings will win at the end.

Another superstition in baseball dates back to the time when beer was the most common and popular drink. If a player passed a load of empty barrels on his way to the ball field, it was considered a sure sign of base hits. An old-time player would tip his hat to them. An amusing tale is told about John McGraw, manager of the Giants, who broke up a disastrous batting slump in his team by using this superstition. One day a player came into the clubhouse smiling broadly; he had just seen a load of empty barrels and was confident that he would break the spell that afternoon. He made four out of a possible five hits. The next day three or four more players saw the barrels, and all made hits leading to the first win in a week. One day two of the players, in comparing notes about the barrels, discovered that they were drawn by the same team of horses, one sorrel and one white. "Sure they were," said McGraw. "I hired that load of empty barrels by the week to drive around and meet you fellows on the way to the park, and you don't think I can afford to have them change horses every day, do you?"

The belief persists that no season should ever be scheduled to start on a Friday. For many years, until it was upset in 1914, there was another firm belief that the team that leads a league on the Fourth of July will win the pennant.

Finally, there is the custom of the seventh-inning stretch, which originated in the days when pine boards without backs were used as seats. The reason everyone rose and stretched at about the seventh inning was to relieve cramped muscles. Then came the superstitious notion that that inning brought good luck to the home team because seven has always been considered the luckiest of all numbers. The custom of standing has become a universal practice wherever and whenever baseball is played.

The prize ring has fully as many superstitions as the baseball game. Boxers have a great belief in the power of charms to ensure victory. They become firmly attached to robes, trunks, and blankets that they have worn in successful fights. Beaten fighters often attribute defeat to their failure to wear a favorite set of trunks or shoes. New shoes are dreaded.

Jack Dempsey, one of the greatest of ring champions, always wore a dingy, faded sweater. He wore it when he became heavyweight champion of the world by defeating Jess Willard in the blazing heat of July, 1919, and two years later he wore it again when he beat Georges Carpentier with a knockout. When he failed to wear it, defending his championship against Luis Firpo, the Wild Bull of the Pampas, he encountered difficulties, and though his boxing was magnificent, he came near to losing his title. Thereafter he always wore the sweater. Gene Tunney was partial to a blue robe bearing the insignia of the United States Marines, and he retired undefeated.

Fighters often carry lucky charms concealed or sewed into their trunks; sometimes these charms are medals, intended to keep away evil in the form of a right cross, an uppercut, or a foul blow. Lightweight Joe Gans always carried one of his pet dice into the ring with him, and Jack Johnson thought a ten-dollar bill tucked into his trunks would ensure his victory. Two prominent heavyweights, Jersey Joe Walcott and Sam Langford, relied on Harlem's traditional lucky piece, a rabbit's foot.

Boxers have hated to climb into the ring first ever since John L. Sullivan, maintaining that the first man in could not win, demanded that the champion be allowed to duck under the ropes after his challenger. In 1892 Sullivan was tricked by the manager of his opponent, Jim Corbett, into entering the ring first. In the twenty-first round—those were the days of long-drawn-out bouts, which were not stopped by referees when one of the fighters was being severely trounced—Corbett knocked him out, the first and only time the unconquerable John L. ever went down for the count.

Boxers hate to see a hat on the bed. After Max Schmeling lost his heavyweight title to Jack Sharkey, a friend came into his dressing room and tossed his hat on the bed. When the fighter's handlers realized that the friend had done this constantly at the training camp, they felt they knew why Schmeling had lost!

In the final round, however, it must be admitted that

both self-confidence and skill are needed to win at boxing. Joe Louis, one of the greatest, was not superstitious at all.

During a horse race jockeys almost always carry their favorite good-luck charms. Trainers, too, exercise great care. They dislike having their horses photographed in the paddock before a race, and many resent being wished good luck and forbid any whistling. Many owners will not bet on their own horses, although this rule often changes when they have a champion.

Jockeys consider it bad luck if their boots touch the floor before a race; they should be left on the shelf on which they are kept until the jockey is ready to put them on. Jockeys worry if they drop a whip while mounting or if the horse snorts while parading to the post.

Football and soccer superstitions tend to include team customs and traditions rather than personal jinxes. Only a player who asks for it ever wears number thirteen, but it is considered lucky to wear the same number in every game. Backfield men will not step on the field lines. Football and soccer players will spit for good luck, which is common among all athletes. This custom dates back to pagan times, when spittle was thought to be the center of power and a potent agent for magic protection. As in baseball the self-confidence of the player must be preserved at all cost, so that winning becomes a habit. The relative lack of superstition in football and soccer is often explained by the fact that in few other sports does teamwork mean as much. In these two sports the individual in subservient to the team.

SPORTS AND SUPERSTITION

Because of the extreme dangers involved, automobile racers invariably carry a lucky charm—baby shoes, goggles, and other talismans—to protect them against disaster. This is the most dangerous of all sports, and more participants are killed or maimed in it than in any other contest. As one writer has expressed it, "With death so frequently pressing a heavy foot on the accelerator pedal, it is no wonder that drivers will believe in anything which may serve to protect them. They literally have contracts with the devil."

Race drivers will never sign autographs or have their pictures taken before a race. They always get into their cars from the side opposite the exhaust pipe.

In their profession they need any and every assurance they can get.

In answer to the question of whether or not professional golfers are superstitious, one would have to say "Yes and No." The Yes is for the British and Scots; the No for the Americans. The reason may be the age of the game. The oldest golf club in the world was founded in England in 1680, almost three centuries ago. The first in America dates back only to 1888. The British have had longer than we have to build up both traditions and superstitions. It has also been suggested that Americans are so set upon winning through superior skill and strength that they have little interest in superstition.

The best-known and most respected British tradition is expressed in the adage "Two up and five to play never won a match." It means that bad luck will come to a player if he happens to be leading an opponent by two holes when there are only five holes left to play. In other words, it predicts the certain defeat of the golfer who walks off the thirteenth green with the match two holes in his favor. The superstition is said to have originated two centuries ago in Scotland. Apparently, some Scotsman, who was two holes up at the thirteenth hole, played badly from thereon and lost the match. This same phenomenon undoubtedly occurred frequently, and it became a sort of mental hazard for players.

In golf the mental side is more important than the physical, and players, aware of this saying, undoubtedly began worrying at the fourteenth hole and were unable to concentrate on their shots over the remainder of the distance. The frequent failures were purely psychological, but the situation finally came to be regarded as an omen of certain disaster. This barrier to victory has been documented in many matches and tournaments.

The other principal superstition states, "He who wins the first hole will lose the match." This superstition is identical with a similar one in poker, that winning the first jackpot is unlucky. Again, enough important games seem to have substantiated the belief that it has gained credence.

Most golfers pay little attention to the bad luck associated with the number thirteen, however. Many good golfers carry thirteen clubs or request locker number thirteen at tournaments or the number thirteen for their caddies. Some carry in their bags a discarded old club that at some time in the past had proved to be lucky.

Other beliefs are observed. Many golfers will not clean the ball when a match is going in their favor, and they will not approach the tee from the front. Among the sure invitations to disaster are changing numbers on the ball, using an opponent's pencil to keep score, changing one's mind about the right club to use after one has been taken from the bag, and using the services of a cross-eyed caddy.

7. Superstition in the Worlds of Music and the Theater

> "I perceive that in all things ye are too superstitious."
> —New Testament, Acts 17:22 (*c.* A.D. 50)

If it were possible to determine the extent of superstitious belief among various professions, musicians and theater people would definitely find a place near the top. By the very nature of their profession actors and actresses are required to express a wide variety of emotions, and by reputation, not deserved in all cases, they are emotional and temperamental. Their world is one of make-believe, and they sometimes carry it over into their offstage lives.

Life in the theater is unstable for all concerned. Productions that fail or have short runs far outnumber the successes, and predictions of success are almost worthless. Many actors suffer from long periods of unemployment between engagements, and box-office receipts may not meet expenses, so that even moderately successful productions are forced to close. This prevailing atmosphere of uncertainty undoubtedly contributes to the high incidence of superstitious belief in the theater. For instance, a large number of actors consult astrologers or the daily forecasts to determine if the stars are propitious; many will not consider making an appointment with a producer, agent, or company manager if the time in their signs appears to be unlucky.

The physical theater itself is often surrounded by beliefs. A certain theater may be considered unlucky or jinxed because of the number of failures it has housed or because unfortunate incidents have occurred there on- or offstage. A superstitious actor is depressed at the prospect of appearing at such a theater, and it is only the insecurity of his profession that forces him to ignore his fears. An owner or manager whose theater has acquired such a reputation may change its name so that his luck will turn.

Everyone in the profession agrees that a cat, even a black one, is a lucky thing to have around a theater. The famous old Haymarket Theatre in London once had a trained black cat "to put the actors in good humor." Because it is lucky, a cat must never be kicked, lest ill fortune result. On the other hand, if by chance the theater cat runs across the stage during a performance, the results will be nothing short of catastrophic.

British actors believe that if the first person to purchase a ticket for a play is an old man or women, the play will have a long run. If the purchaser is young, the omen is bad. Actors often check on this personally so they will be prepared.

Because of the universality of the superstition regarding the number thirteen, many theaters do not identify the first row as A, in which case M would be readily identified as the thirteenth. Instead, the first and second rows are labeled AA and BB, followed by row A. Large theaters use the double alphabet for the first twenty-six rows in the hope that the thirteenth row will not be easily identified. In each instance, the patron who wants to avoid anything having to do with that fatal number will probably not discover the ruse. Seats numbered thirteen are more easily avoided by alert ticket purchasers.

Before a performance it is unlucky for an usher to seat the first patron to arrive if that patron happens to hold a ticket numbered thirteen. In such a case, bad luck will follow and the usher will encounter many difficulties during the rest of the seating. Similarly, bad luck will follow if the usher does not hear the first words of the play. In England, where programs are sold, it is unlucky for the usher if a women tips her but not if a man does. The first tip received at the beginning of a new season or play should not be spent; the usher should rub it against her leg and then keep it in her pocket for the rest of the run to ensure that many others will follow.

In stage settings and during the action of a play, there are at least three conditions to be avoided. Real flowers should never be used because they are very unlucky for both the actors and the production. Only artificial flowers should be used in decorating a scene or should be worn by a performer. The restriction is partially due to the fear that an actor may inadvertently brush his costume against a vase filled with water, with humiliating results. The taboo does not, of course, apply to bouquets presented to actresses over the footlights at the end of the performance, because they have no part in the play.

A standard superstition, still believed in England but no longer observed in the United States, concerns peacock tail feathers. Actors believe that the presence of either the tail feathers or any representation of the bird itself on the stage will cause the play to be a failure or make something go seriously wrong during the run. This taboo applies to designs used in stage sets or on curtains, and even to carvings on pieces of furniture. It had its origin in the traditional belief that the open eyes on the feathers, a prominent part of their design, represented the evil eye, and therefore constituted one of the worst forms of bad luck.

Most actors and stage and costume designers consider the color yellow unlucky, mainly because it becomes bland under the lights. Actors prefer bold colors that will make them stand out.

In their dressing rooms superstitious actors scrupulously avoid certain portents of bad luck. Whistling anywhere in the theater, but particularly in a dressing room, is considered the most dangerous act possible, for it indicates that someone, not necessarily the whistler, will become unemployed. Many actors firmly believe that they will be given two weeks' notice, the traditional warning, if someone whistles in their presence or, if the dressing room is shared, that the actor nearest the door will be discharged. If the whistler is a fellow actor, he is put out at once and made to turn around three times outside before being readmitted. This is supposed to break the spell. One explanation of the origin of this whistling superstition goes back to biblical times, when unfeeling women supposedly stood by whistling while they watched workmen forging the nails for Christ's cross.

The makeup box is an actor's most valuable possession. A true professional never carries his makeup box, for doing so would bring bad luck; only the most inexperienced amateur would do that. A makeup box must never be in good order; luck comes to the actor who leaves it cluttered. A popular belief of chorus girls is that if powder is dropped on the floor, it should be danced upon before being removed.

If, when an actor kicks his shoes off in a dressing room, they fall upright, it is a lucky sign, but if they fall over on their sides or if he or anyone else puts them on a chair, bad luck will follow.

An actor should not look into a dressing-table mirror over the shoulder of another, so that the two reflections are seen together. To do this brings certain misfortune to the one in front.

During the all-important rehearsals for a new play, several superstitions are studiously observed. When the cast and staff assemble for the first reading, they must never number thirteen. If they do, a stagehand or auditor must be summoned to sit in as a nonparticipant. During the rehearsals there should never by any applause from either members or auditors. Professional actors fear that if a rehearsal is quite perfect, it is a sign that the play will fare badly when it is produced or that it will have only a short run. Nor should anyone quote any of the text of the play in offstage conversation. The actor speaking the last, or tag, line must never speak it during rehearsal; it must not be spoken until opening night.

The most harrowing fear of actors and actresses is that accidents will occur during a performance, creating situations that will make them appear ridiculous. The laughter of an audience can upset the subsequent scene or the entire play. Nervous players are often haunted by dreams of such mishaps. The most potent belief is that if a costume catches onto a piece of scenery or an entrance door sticks and will not open, the rest of the performance will go badly. Actresses with long trains in period plays are always alert, lest their trains be stepped upon or become tangled, for kicking them straight cannot go unnoticed by an audience. Billowing or hoop skirts also present such difficulties, and can be fatal to the smoothness of the action.

A rabbit's foot is preferred as a personal mascot, particularly one that was presented by an admirer on opening night. An actor should never be wished "Good luck" before going on stage. Instead of uttering that phrase or crossing the fingers, one should say something insulting—"May you break your leg!" is the most frequent wish. The purpose is to confuse the evil spirits that are waiting to trap a performer.

The first entrance of an actor is most crucial, for any mishap will spoil the success of the rest of the play. If an actor trips as he makes his first entrance, the belief is that he will miss a cue or forget his lines at some time during the performance, unless he is able to retrace his steps and make a fresh start. In contrast to stumbling, a fall, though dreaded because it makes the actor look ridiculous, causes an audience to feel sympathetic, and therefore foretells a good performance and a long and successful engagement. One unusual belief is that an actor with squeaking shoes is sure to make a successful first entrance.

Actors often dislike three candles on a stage or in a dressing room because the candles indicate that there will be a quarrel.

Knitting by actresses onstage is taboo in English productions. However, to find a piece of yarn or thread that will wind around the finger without breaking indicates that a good contract will be signed with a prominent actor or manager. That actor's or manager's last name will begin with the letter suggested by the number of times the thread goes around the finger. For example, three times means the letter C.

The horror of all concerned with the theater is that a woman might faint or a patron become ill or even die in the audience while a play is in progress. That is considered an ill omen of the worst sort.

English actors believe that Shakespeare's *Macbeth* is very unlucky, and that lines from it must never be spoken offstage, even in readings. A universal belief in the theater is that it is such an exceedingly unlucky play that any presentation of it is almost sure to be marked by a series of misfortunes affecting members of the cast or anyone associated with the production. The reason given is that the witches' song in *Macbeth* possesses the power to work evil. Many true stories are told of accidents, some of them serious, outbreaks of fire, and other troubles that have occurred in various British theaters while the play was running.

This persistent belief concerning *Macbeth* was based on two riots during performances, one in London and one in New York City, during the first half of the nineteenth century, when Shakespearean actors and plays enjoyed great popularity.

One of the most distinguished families ever to appear on the English stage—comparable to the Barrymores in the United States early in the twentieth century—was the Kembles. In 1803 John Kemble became manager of London's famous Covent Garden Theatre, in which members of the family appeared for five years. Then it was completely destroyed by a disastrous fire in 1808. In the true theatrical tradition that "the show must go on," the theater was completely rebuilt within a year, and the prices raised to cover the expense of the construction. The opening performance, on September 18, 1809, was *Macbeth,* with three of the Kembles in leading roles—John in the title role, a younger brother, Charles, as Macduff, and their sister, the "incomparable" Sarah Kemble Siddons, considered to be the greatest actress that ever lived, in her most famous role as Lady Macbeth.

Before the performance began John Kemble made an address of welcome, but he could not be heard. Suddenly, the audience began to chant, "Old prices! Old prices! Old prices!"

The curtain was rung up, but the shouting and abuse continued. Not even the appearance of the beloved Mrs.

Siddons could quiet the house. None of the lines in the five acts of the play could be heard above the din.

That was the start of the Old Price Riots, a siege that lasted for the incredible length of sixty-six evenings. Night after night a play in the repertory would begin, and the audience would perhaps listen to the first and second acts in silence. Then an uproar would break out. People would run up and down the aisles shouting, making noise with rattles and bells, and staging fights. There were such howling mobs at each performance that the police could not control them.

The Covent Garden Theatre could not be operated at the former prices without a loss, but the crowds refused to recognize that fact. The wages earned by the poorer people in the upper galleries were barely enough to keep them alive, and the Kemble family was used as the focus of their protest.

Because of the continuing disruptions, the aristocrats and wealthy people, who were willing to pay higher admission prices, stopped coming to the performances. In the middle of December John Kemble finally surrendered; the former prices, he announced in a curtain speech, would be put back. This first curse of *Macbeth* was to be remembered.

Several decades later in the United States, additional misfortune resulted when *Macbeth* was performed, the cause being American antipathy toward the English. This antipathy was reflected in what was called the Nativist movement. However, the trouble was sparked by a feud between William Macready, an eminent English tragedian, and his equally noted American rival, Edwin Forrest. The feud originated in 1847, when Forrest hissed continuously and talked and laughed loudly during an Edinburgh performance of *Hamlet* starring Macready. When Macready made a preretirement tour of the United States, beginning in the fall of 1848, he encountered similar noisy opposition wherever he went. In a Philadelphia performance of *Macbeth* in October, a section of the audience hissed and booed continuously and threw rotten eggs onto the stage.

On his arrival in New York at the end of his tour, Macready felt the full force of the anti-English feelings. In what was no mere coincidence, Forrest had scheduled *Macbeth* on Monday, May 7, 1849, Macready's opening night, with the same play at the Astor Place Opera House. The newspapers encouraged public interest in the "the great theatrical warfare which has been rising to fever heat."

During Macready's performance the actors were completely inaudible because of the shouts and hisses of the audience, and the stage was pelted with rotten eggs, pennies, vegetables, and fruits. A shower of pieces of broken chairs finally caused Macready to discontinue the performance before the third act. Undaunted, however, he agreed to perform again on Thursday evening, May 10. Forrest changed his schedule so that he would also play *Macbeth* on the tenth.

The stage was set for disaster. Three hundred police were assigned inside the Opera House and on the adjoining streets. Those outside were reinforced by two hundred soldiers of the Seventh Infantry Regiment, cavalry and light artillery, the latter supplied with two cannons.

The uproar began when Macready made his first entrance. When several ringleaders were arrested and other disturbers were escorted into the street, it was the signal for violence unparalleled in theatrical history. People began to hurl stones and bricks from a sewer construction site through the windows of the theater into the orchestra seats. A fire was set in the basement. Meanwhile, the crowd outside battered on the doors hoping to force them open.

The crowd was estimated to number from ten to twenty thousand people. Many policemen were wounded when they attempted to disperse the mob, and they sought refuge inside. The cavalry unit was ordered to move against the crowd, but was met with a hail of stones and brickbats. The infantry then attempted to clear the area closest to the building, around which a cordon of police protected the audience as they left at the end of the performance.

When the soldiers began to force back the pressing mob at bayonet point, the crowd reacted with increased fury. The general in command ordered the rioters to fall back or they would be fired upon, but the answer was a concerted rush. The soldiers fired over their heads. When that proved ineffective, because the rioters thought the shots were blanks instead of bullets, the soldiers opened fire directly into the crowd. Three successive volleys resulted in deaths and injuries. The crowd dispersed only when the two cannons were hauled up and aimed at them.

The most reliable estimate of casualties was 31 killed and 150 wounded. Macready was able to leave the theater under police guard, and this tragic *Macbeth* was his final performance in America. He was smuggled out of the city the next day and sailed from Boston a fortnight later, never to return.

In 1946 tragedy struck again, when the magnificent new National Theater in Lisbon, Portugal, burned to the ground a few hours after a performance of *Macbeth*.

The belief of Shakespearean actors that *Macbeth* is an unlucky play may have some basis in view of its tragic history.

Superstition has not become attached to music quite as much as it has to the theater. Still, Franz Joseph Haydn would never compose without wearing a ring that was given to him after a performance at court, and the composers Chopin and Rossini both believed in the power of the number thirteen. So did Arnold Schönberg, the Austrian composer. Born on September 13, 1874, Schönberg professed a conviction that he would also die on the thirteenth, which he did, on July 13, 1951, a few hours after he had asked his wife the date.

Richard Wagner also believed implicitly that the number thirteen had a special significance for him: His name contained thirteen letters; he was born in 1813; when his opera *Tannhäuser* was first performed on March 13, 1845, it was not a success, though later it was widely praised, and he died on February 13, 1883.

Coincidence played an obvious part in the cases of Schönberg and Wagner, but such singular occurrences as these cannot be lightly dismissed by the true believer in superstition.

Memory sometimes fails a performer. When a superstitious musician, vocal or instrumental, encounters difficulty in a composition, he believes he should stop and begin all over again; this belief corresponds to the belief about the bad entrance of an actor. A variation is that the singer or musician must not resume the same piece, but start something new. There is some common sense in this belief, because when the mood of the performer has been broken, he is not likely to recapture it. That is also why most singers render a new song when encored. Clara Schumann, the pianist noted for her interpretations of Chopin's works, always played from memory, but she sat on the music! An English superstition states that if a member of a church choir sings a false note in an anthem, his Sunday dinner will be scorched.

Black magic has played a part in the folklore of music. It is found in the voyage of Odysseus in the Greek *Odyssey* (and of Ulysses in the Latin version); when the Sirens attempted to lure the hero and his crew with their songs, the hero had himself tied to the mast, and ordered his crew to stop their ears with wax so they would not succumb. In German mythology the parallel is the Lorelei, a Rhine maiden who lived on a cliff above the river and with her singing lured unwary boatmen to their deaths on the rocks below.

When the black art in music pertains to the male, it is in the guise of the devil. Some of the famous early violinists were thought to be in league with the devil. The almost superhuman playing of both Giuseppe Tartini and Niccolò Paganini, eighteenth-century Italian violinists, was attributed to such a league. Tartini's *Devil's Trill Sonata* was popularly supposed to have been inspired by Satan. The evil effect of music was supposedly exhibited during the 1940's in the tune "Gloomy Sunday," which was later played on the zither as the theme song of an Orson Welles film, *The Third Man*. This melancholy composition originated in Budapest and was reputedly the cause of so many suicides that its performance was prohibited by the Hungarian government.

Opera, a form of theater, shares many of the theater's superstitions. A black cat in an opera house, however, is considered to be unlucky, although, as in the theater, whistling backstage and peacock feathers and live flowers on stage are forbidden. European singers, especially Italians and Spaniards, sometimes believe that their understudies, or alternates, have put the evil eye on them in order to take over their roles.

In the different opera houses of the world, many strange good-luck rituals are performed backstage before a singer makes his first entrance. In the wings waiting to go onstage, opera singers, unlike actors, are not sent off with the curse "May you break your leg!" The ritual is much more detailed. In a German or Austrian opera house someone is likely to swing a singer around and spit vigorously three times on his left shoulder or to administer a vigorous kick. Germans may say *"Hals und Beinbruch,"* which means "Break your neck and legs"; they may also say *"Alles Schlechte"* ("Everything bad"). The French counterpart is to whisper *"Merde,"* an extremely vulgar word. But of all the expressions and gestures, none is more meaningful to the singer than the Italian phrase *"In bocca al lupo"* ("Into the wolf's mouth"), which signifies that as a singer moves onstage, he steps into the mouth of the wolf, the audience; the singer either succeeds or is eaten.

Among prominent opera stars, Enrico Caruso, considered to be the greatest of all tenors, was extremely superstitious. Highly emotional, he constantly felt that he was threatened with disaster. In her biography of him, his wife, Dorothy, reported that he was afraid of women hunchbacks, and that he never passed under a ladder or wore a new suit on a Friday. Neither would he depart or arrive on a Friday. At one time he asserted that a series of minor accidents that had occurred during three days was due to an interviewer who had an evil eye (a *iettatore*), at another that the presence of his voice coach during performances of *Carmen* jinxed his singing of the high and difficult B flat at the end of the "Flower Song."

Like *Macbeth* on the dramatic stage, some operas are considered to be jinxed, bringing misfortune to all concerned. For example, *The Tales of Hoffmann,* with its hypnotist and unlucky diamond, was not immediately successful and was infrequently performed. Later it had a resounding and lasting success. Individual opera singers may sometimes refuse to perform a role in which they have not been well received.

One of the operas dogged by superstition was a minor work of the French composer Jacques Halévy, best known for *La Juive.* His opera *Charles VI* came to be dreaded by singers. The famous French tenor Jean Etienne Auguste Massol sang the title role, but on three successive nights someone in the audience dropped dead after he had sung his principal aria, "O God, kill him!"—first a stagehand, then a prominant boxholder, and finally the conductor of the orchestra.

The opera was discontinued for nine years, partly because Massol refused to sing the role again and partly for political reasons. It was feared that the subject of the opera might affect France's current diplomatic relations with England.

Nine years later, in 1858, Emperor Napoleon III ordered a revival of the opera, with Massol again singing the title role. The Emperor and Empress Eugénie were to attend the performance on January 14, and a distinguished audience awaited their arrival. On the way to the opera house, however, Napoleon's coach was bombed by an Italian anarchist, Felice Orsini, and although the Emperor was unharmed, several other people were killed. The opera was not performed that evening, nor did anybody later attempt to prove the absurdity of the superstition. *Charles VI* passed into obscurity.

8. Foretelling the Future

"What is past I know, but what is to come I know not."
—Apocrypha, 2 Esdras, 4:46 (A.D. 100)

What is past is finished, or, as Shakespeare's Macbeth said, "What's done is done." On the other hand, the future is a mystery that must be faced.

Fortune-telling, the practice of foretelling the future or destiny of an individual, is as old as mankind itself. Soothsayers, seers, and prophets observed natural phenomena, "seeing" in them the forecasts of coming events, and arrived at conclusions that guided the future actions of high and low alike. Later the varied skills of fortune-telling were organized into specific systematic practices and skills.

FORETELLING THE FUTURE

The extent of belief in and reliance on fortune-telling is difficult to determine. In the United States the only available evidence is in the thousands, even millions, of copies of books and periodicals that relate to fortune-telling and in the large number of practitioners located everywhere. In England, however, Geoffrey Gorer made a survey of superstitious belief in the early 1950's, using the replies of five thousand readers of the *People,* one of the largest Sunday newspapers. Most of these respondents were over thirty-five years of age. Their answers to his questionnaire and a follow-up field study offer concrete evidence of belief in fortune-telling.*

1. *Have you ever been to a professional fortune-teller?*
   Yes 44%, No 53%, No answer 3%

2. *If yes, how often have you been?*
   Once 45%, Twice 24%, No answer 31%

3. *Did any of it come true?*
   Yes 30%, Yes, all 2%, Yes, some 15%, No, nothing 35%, Don't know 11%, No answer 7%

Mr. Gorer offered further revealing information on these questions. Probably many people go to a fortune-teller once in their lives "just for luck." Two thirds of the men and a third of the women admitted that they had. Apparently, they considered it an amusing and harmless diversion, not to be taken seriously as an infallible and trustworthy guide to the future. Nevertheless, approximately a fifth of the men and a fourth of the women had

*Source: Geoffrey Gorer, *Exploring English Character.* London, Barrie & Jenkins, 1955, pp. 266-267, 469-472 (tables).

two consultations. Seven percent of the total were more frequent addicts, and about half of those who consulted a fortune-teller—that is, a fifth of the total—believed that the predictions had come true in whole or in part. Fortune-telling, then, is apparently accepted by a large number of Englishmen.

One of the most popular forms of fortune-telling is with cards, the technical name for which is cartomancy. The origin of playing cards is shrouded in the past. They can be traced back to India by way of Persia and Egypt, and were originally designed to foretell the future. Whatever their origin, they were brought to Europe by tribes of Gypsies wandering from India sometime during the fourteenth century. The oldest pack of cards dates back to the one owned by Charles VI of France in 1392; it is still on display in a Paris museum and is the ancestor of the standard playing-card deck used today.

The packs used by Gypsies were called tarots and consisted of seventy-eight cards. Of these, fifty-six were suit cards similar to those in modern packs, except that the suits were swords, cups, coins, and rods, with four court cards—king, queen, knight, and knave (jack). The additional twenty-two cards had symbolic meanings, such as love, justice, fortune, strength, and death.

The tarot cards are supposed to reveal the secrets of man and the universe interpreted in terms of the past, present, and future. The way the cards fall when they are laid out for reading and their relation to one another reveal to the trained reader facts about some of the important concerns in the life of the subject. Some cards foretell good, others bad. For instance, the ace pertains to the home and happiness, and the ten of jacks promises success and good luck in any project, or a pleasant surprise.

The standard fifty-two-card deck is used more often than tarot cards today. The method is simpler because each of the four suits has a certain significance. Two suits are positive and two negative. Clubs portend happiness, ability in money matters, power, fame, and good omens. Hearts signify joy and love. The "bad" cards are diamonds, which denote delay, quarrels, and annoyances, and spades, the worst, which foretell misfortunes such as grief, sickness, loss of money, enemies, and treachery.

In addition, each card in the deck has its own specific meaning. The nine of hearts, for instance, is a wish card. The nine of spades means grief and sickness; the nine of clubs, unexpected gain or a legacy; and the nine of diamonds, annoyance and delay. Cards turned up in groups also have special meanings. All of this knowledge helps an experienced reader, whether professional or amateur, to make specific predictions.

The oriental counterpart of the tarot is *I Ching*, the ancient Chinese *Book of Changes*, which contains methods and explanations of prophecy. With these instructions the correct course of action can be obtained by tossing sticks or coins. The book contains sixty-four hexagrams (six-pointed starlike figures), which are interpreted according to the fall of a coin. For example, if the toss results in the number sixty, the symbol in the book is restraint. As interpreted, it means that any plans should be undertaken with the utmost care and deliberation, and no decision should be made without cautious planning. A reading might include such statements as "You must act from your knowledge of the right time, when plans can be carried through and when they will not be blocked" and "Persistence in the right course will bring good fortune and freedom from error." These interpretations should, of course, be put into action.

Fortune-telling with dice originated in India, where it is called *ramala*. An inquirer is expected to have a definite question in mind when he throws the eight dice. The numbers that appear are interpreted according to the rules contained in a series of ancient books.

Teacup reading, called tasseography, is one of the simplest and most entertaining forms of amateur fortune-telling. Professionally it is undertaken especially by Gypsies. The tea should be brewed in a teapot without a strainer, obviously because sufficient leaves must pour into the cup for reading. When the tea has been drunk, the cup is placed upside down on the saucer and turned around three times. The leaves that drop into the saucer show the past, and those that stay in the cup tell the future.

The reader interprets the shapes and forms that are made by the leaves and their distribution on the cup, whether around the sides, on the rim, or on the bottom. For example, a leaf on the rim represents the present time and indicates that something is happening currently. Small specks are the symbols for money; a shape like a pair of shoes means a trip. A long stem represents a man, a short stem, a woman. Long wavy lines denote losses and vexations; straight ones foretell peace and a long life. The meanings of the shapes—triangles, crowns, leaves, animals, flowers, hearts, and mountains—are almost endless. Coffee grounds can be used instead of tea leaves, but the results are poor because they cannot form as many symbols as tea leaves.

An occult method of revealing future happenings is crystal gazing, called crystallomancy. By looking into the ball, or scrying, the gazer achieves a clairvoyant state and is able to see distinct happenings and future events.

Palmistry is a type of fortune-telling that involves foretelling events and analyzing character from the shape and lines of the hands, fingers, and nails. Though not as popular as astrology, palmistry, which has been described as "the diagramming of the hand into lines and mounts, with the fidelity of explorers," is accepted by many as reliable truth today. Before reading the hands, a Gypsy usually crosses the palm of the subject with a silver coin, to bring luck and good fortune in her reading.

The revelations interpreted by palm reading are very specific. A hand that is thick and coarse, with short fingers, for example, is taken to indicate a brutal and unimaginative character. A hand square in shape suggests industry and honest dealings. A palm with fingers tapering from a broad base suggests a witty, social, and artistic person. One that is fan-shaped, with fingers spread at the top, reveals a daring and energetic spirit. A hand bony and irregular in shape, with protruding joints, suggests a character adept at dealing with knotty problems. A "mixed" hand, one with a combination of characteristics, suggests an unpredictable and complex personality. The details are "read" by the palmist.

The fatty areas, called mounts, and their locations at the base of the fingers give the clue to character traits. Each has a particular significance. Lines on the hand are held to be important indications of life and traits of character. If the line representing life, for example, is long, a person will live to a ripe old age. Broken lines indicate accidents or illnesses, and eventually death. Other lines concern love, ambition, fate, health, success, and failure.

Palmistry has a long history and continues to attract the credulous. Many of those who consult palmists feel that their analyses are more valid than other forms of fortune-telling.

In two American studies the percentage of people who had faith in palmistry was fifty-three and fifty, indicating that half the population has confidence in its revelations. Two other American studies indicated that women place more faith in palmistry than men.

Astrology (from the Greek, meaning the science of the stars) is based on the theory that the stars influence human affairs and determine the course of events. In astrology a belt in the heavens, called the zodiac, is divided into twelve sections, or signs, of about thirty days each. The day you were born the sun was in one of these sections of the sky, and that became the sign that is said to determine your characteristics and the events that will influence your life. When a chart, or horoscope, is prepared, based on your zodiacal sign and the location of the planets at the time of your birth, predictions can be made about your future actions, conduct, and affairs.

Astrologers do not confine their forecasts to the immediate concerns of individuals, but also predict future events regarding political issues, economic problems, and other problems of public interest. In such cases successful projections are likely to impress people and to be remembered and the failures are soon forgotten. If the number of times predictions have failed to come true is considered, the successes can often be explained by chance—or advance information on the part of the forecaster, since general tendencies in the stock market or in political affairs, for example, are often known beforehand.

Astrology today is by far the most accepted and believed form of forecasting the future. In both the United States and Great Britain, predictions are followed in varying degrees by millions of people. Though it is discredited and dismissed as rubbish in academic circles, professional astrologers consider astrology to be a science, and indeed, there is some truth in this contention because of the methods used.

Astrological lore is very old, and the extensive knowledge that the ancient Egyptians, Babylonians, Assyrians, and Chaldeans had concerning it was gained because of the belief in the divine influence of heavenly bodies. Astrology was popular in ancient Greece in the fourth century B.C., and later it was much studied by the Romans ("the ides of March" of Julius Caesar, for example), even after it was officially prohibited. In the Middle Ages it was associated with alchemy (the science of transforming ordinary metals into gold) and other occult sciences, and prepared the way for the modern science of astronomy. After the work of Copernicus, Galileo, and other pioneers of astronomy, astrology became a separate area of learning.

Its revival in the twentieth century has been marked by an interest that can truly be termed phenomenal. Psychologists aver that this has been due to the complexities of modern life and their effects on individuals.

In 1971, 10,000 professional and 175,000 part-time astrologers were reported to be active in the United States. Daily horoscopes appeared in 1,200 of America's 1,750 daily newspapers, with a total readership of forty million. In 1969 an estimated twenty million Americans spent more than $150 million on personal horoscope material and $35 million on pamphlets and books.

Regularly scheduled television and radio programs are devoted to astrology, and computerized horoscopes are purchased by the hundreds of thousands in the United States and France. According to a study Max Gunther made of stock-market investors in New York City during the late 1960's, an amazing number of them depended on astrological forecasts in determining what stocks they should purchase. One of America's most noted astrologists, Carroll Righter, has published an astrological guide to the stock market for every day that the exchanges are open for a year.

Every two thousand years the earth is said to enter a new astrological phase, named for one of the zodiacal symbols, and mankind is influenced by its meaning. Some astrologers say we are now in the Age of Aquarius, or the generation of Aquarius, which reached its peak on February 4, 1962. Other astrologers, who disagree on the boundaries of the signs of the zodiac, say the Age of Aquarius will not start until the next century.

The predecessor to Aquarius, the Piscean Age, has been a melancholy era filled with bloodshed and chaos. The new age began, or will begin, with the sun, moon, Mars, Venus, Jupiter, Mercury, and Saturn all in the sign of Aquarius for the first time in centuries. It is supposed to bring "an advance toward universal brotherhood, enlightenment, and greater freedom for all mankind." It will be welcome.

9. Predicting the Weather

> A pupil in a many-chambered school
> Where superstition weaves her airy dreams.
> —William Wordsworth, *The Excursion* (1814)

Ancient man was terrified by the forces of nature, because he did not understand them. To him climate and weather were unsolved mysteries. He thought demons brought bad weather and beneficent gods fair weather. Throughout the ages, however, those whose lives were most affected by weather—farmers, shepherds, hunters, and sailors—translated their observations into codes or proverbs, and some of them have come down to us from the earliest times. Many of the ancient proverbs are evidence of keen observation and the result of tested experience. Through them it is possible to predict weather with some accuracy. Other sayings are true only in a very limited sense, and some have no scientific foundation whatever and are completely false.

Weather proverbs vary somewhat in different countries; one that may be fairly accurate in one country may not apply in another, because of varying winds, ocean currents, mountain barriers, and other geographical factors. The saying that an east wind brings rain and a wind from the northwest indicates fair weather is a good forecast for many parts of North America. In a country like Israel, however, the opposite is true: A wind from the west is usually moist (from the Mediterranean), and one from the east is hot and dry.

The latter observation is included in the Bible: "An east wind shall come, the wind of the Lord shall come up from the wilderness, and his spring shall become dry, and his fountain shall be dried up" (Hos. 13:15); "the east wind brought the locusts" (Exod. 10:13); and "When ye see a cloud rise out of the west, straightway ye say, There cometh a shower; and so it is (Luke 12:54).

Certain weather proverbs are based on the appearance of the sky, whose colors roughly indicate the amount of moisture and dust present in the atmosphere. The colors of the sky are best observed when the sun is near the horizon, that is, at sunrise and sunset. The latter was mentioned around the time of Christ in the Gospel According to St. Matthew: "When it is evening, ye say, It will be fair weather: for the sky is red. And in the morning, It will be foul weather to-day: for the sky is red and lowering" (Matt. 16:2-3). The same idea is recorded in an old rhyme:

> Sky red in the morning
> Is a sailor's sure warning:
> Sky red at night
> Is the sailor's delight.

When the sun sets clear and the evening sky is red, it indicates that the atmosphere is relatively dry, and that there is dust in the air. On the other hand, when it is gray, it indicates that much moisture has collected around the dust particles in the air, and conditions are favorable for rain:

> Evening red and morning gray
> Help the traveler on his way;
> Evening gray and morning red
> Bring down rain upon his head.

The saying "Rain before seven stops before eleven" is merely a way of stating that an all-night rain will probably stop before noon.

Rain signs are many, and the appearance of the sun and moon furnishes evidence of a coming rainfall. A red sun is a sign of moisture in the air, with considerable dust in the atmosphere, leading to such expressions as "A red sun has water in his eye" and "If red the sun begins his race, be sure the rain will fall apace."

For the moon, there is the saying "The moon, her face if red be, of water speaks she." A ring around the moon has often been regarded as a sure sign of rain. The small, scattered clouds composed of minute crystals of ice and snow will melt with the rising of the sun, thus causing rain.

A favorite maxim of our ancestors was "If the sun shines while it is raining, there will be rain again tomorrow." That is not necessarily true, because changes in temperature, humidity, and pressure may occur and make the rain impossible.

When a rainbow is seen in the east, the rain or shower is said to be over, while a rainbow in the west is regarded as an indication of rain. This is true, since most clouds travel eastward; a rainbow in the west indicates that clouds are forming and that the rain has not yet passed.

Many rain predictions are based upon the behavior of animals. The following are among the most frequently observed by farmers:

If donkeys bray more than usual and shake their ears, it is a sign of rain:

> When the ass begins to bray
> We surely shall have rain that day.

or

> When the donkey blows his horn
> 'Tis time to house your hay and corn.

Restless and uneven croaking of frogs means that rain is on the way, as is the restless grouping together of toads. If chickens in the barnyard are unusually noisy, if moles build up their hills, if horses stretch their necks, sniff the air, and huddle together in the corner of a field, if rats or mice become active and squeak, and if dogs become sleepy and eat grass, showers are sure to follow.

Crows flying aimlessly to and fro and giving a peculiar caw, not their usual one, also herald the coming of rain. The screeching of the owl, the loud singing of the thrush, and birds in general picking their feathers and flying to their nests are all signs of an approaching storm.

The ant, too, figures as a prophet of rain. A common belief, of course, is that "stepping on an ant brings rain." Unusual activity on the ants' part is a sign; before a storm they carry their eggs to a safe place lest they be washed away. Insects, particularly flies and mosquitoes, seem to bite and sting with more intensity when a siege of rainy weather is at hand.

Dew is the subject of both British and American sayings. The English version is simple: "Morn dry, rain night; morn wet, no rain yet." The American version goes:

> When the dew is on the grass,
> Rain will never come to pass.
> When grass is dry at morning light,
> Look for rain before the night.

A heavy dew in the evening is the best promise of a dry morrow. Dry grass at night or at sunrise indicates rain before noon.

People with rheumatism and arthritis often say it will soon rain when they feel more than ordinary pain in their joints. Sudden changes in the weather do produce certain effects upon the human body. For instance, a decrease in atmospheric pressure or a rise in humidity seems to increase the feeling of pain in the joints. A prediction of this sort may have some justification, therefore, although it certainly is not dependable.

Before forecasting was developed into a science, farmers and amateur weather prophets in both England and the United States predicted the weather for each day by remembering what the weather was like on that same day in the past. The most continously recognized days of this sort have been the European Candlemas Day (February 2) for the coming of spring and the English Saint Swithin's Day (July 15) for summer weather.

On each Candlemas Day the hedgehog, who has been asleep in his burrow since the latter part of October or early November, is supposed to come out of his winter hibernation to inspect the weather. When he emerges, the winter has not yet ended, and spring is generally far in the future; but the Old World tradition is that if the day is cloudy and the sun does not shine, the hedgehog will stay outside and not return to his winter quarters. According to the superstition, he instinctively knows that spring has come to stay. If, however, the day is clear and sunny, so that he sees his shadow, he realizes that the winter is not yet over. Therefore he returns to his winter quarters for another six weeks, during which bad weather and winter will continue. The superstition has been the subject of a traditional rhyme:

> If Candlemas Day be fair and bright,
> Winter will have another flight.
> But if Candlemas Day brings clouds and rain,
> Winter is gone and won't come again.

In the United States the belief refers to the groundhog

(woodchuck), since no animal like the hedgehog exists in America. For several hundred years weather almanacs in both Europe and the United States have alerted their readers to watch for this portent.

Annually, in both countries journalists watch for this sign on no other basis than the old superstition and report the results to a gullible public, for many people have long accepted it as a natural law. Although they have never seen a hedgehog or a groundhog, and it has not even been conclusively proved that groundhogs come from their dens on February 2, many people firmly believe in this fictitious story. They have been told that it is true or have read about it in the daily press, and that helps keep the old tradition alive.

In their *Do You Believe It?* psychologists Otis W. Caldwell and Gerhard Lundeen proved the fallacy of the groundhog superstition. They stated flatly that it could not possibly apply to the northern part of the United States because February 2 is always far from the beginning of spring, winter continuing at least until mid-March. "It is obvious that February 2 may be a cloudy day in some places, yet clear in others not far distant," they wrote, "and according to the old proverb, these localities should experience strikingly different types of weather for the six weeks immediately following Groundhog Day. This is often not found to be the case." They studied government weather records for February and March, 1933 (when the research was undertaken), in eight cities throughout the country. In four of them the weather was clear on February 2, and in four it was cloudy.

In this study the investigators also belittled the saying

PREDICTING THE WEATHER

"When March comes in like a lamb, it goes out like a lion" and the reverse, "If March comes in like a lion, it goes out like a lamb."

The English superstition that if it rains on July 15 (Saint Swithin's Day), there will be rain on each of the following forty days offers an interesting and striking example of how some false beliefs may arise. The proverb is presented in the following jingle:

> Saint Swithin's Day, if thou dost rain,
> For forty days it will remain;
> Saint Swithin's Day, if thou be fair,
> For forty days 'twill rain nae mair [no more].

This superstition had its origin in the canonization of Saint Swithin, a bishop of Winchester, England, who lived during the ninth century. According to his wishes, he was buried outside the church, in the churchyard, where the water from the eaves might drop upon his grave. A century later, when he was canonized, his remains were to be moved to a shrine in the new cathedral. The work of the removal was scheduled to begin on July 15, 971, but it was postponed because, according to the legend, rain fell without interruption for forty days. At that time weather phenomena were often attributed to supernatural agencies, and many people deduced that the prolonged rainy period was sent by the saint to voice his disapproval of the transfer, in violation of his wishes.

In the latter part of the nineteenth century W. C. Plenderleath, a British meteorologist, investigated official weather records with reference to this legendary belief and published the results in a scholarly scientific journal. His results were corroborated by the government meteorological office: If the year is divided into periods of forty days, there are two such periods in which the weather is more constant than in all the others. The most marked of these periods is the forty days that follow Saint Swithin's Day. That is to say, this period is more generally wet or more generally fair than any similar period during the year. Therefore, the legend of Saint Swithin probably evolved simply because the period of settled weather, wet or fine, began around the time of the saint's day.

In the United States within recent years, much attention has been paid to the saying that the amount of brown on the middle band of a woolly bear, a type of caterpillar, foretells the severity of the coming winter. If the band is narrow, the winter will be bad, but if it is wide, the winter will be mild.

This legend dates back to colonial times, but was not scientifically tested until the present century. In the fall of 1947 Dr. C. H. Curran of the American Museum of Natural History went to a rural area and found that, of several caterpillars' eleven segments, only four were brown, a very narrow band. That winter New York had its worst recorded snowstorm in over seventy-five years. In a further check the next year, Dr. Curran reported that the woolly bears had more brown segments, which meant a moderate winter; he was right again. In 1949 the bands were again wide, and another mild winter followed. Measuring the largest number of caterpillars, sixty, in 1950, he found that the woolly bears had six brown segments. Early in November *Life* magazine published a photograph of one of these caterpillars magnified nine times life-size. The winter corroborated the prediction of the photograph by again being mild.

After this four-year accuracy record, the *New York Herald Tribune,* which had given annual page-one coverage to the story, editorialized, "The woolly bear has effectively replaced that tattered perennial, the groundhog."

Rain was and is, of course, an absolute necessity to man, and primitive and near-primitive tribes have always had ceremonies or charms to attract it. Many of these ceremonies are described in detail by Sir James Frazer, a Scottish anthropologist, whose *Golden Bough,* first published in 1890, was a pioneer study in magic and religion. In a chapter titled "The Magical Control of the Weather," Frazer offered a worldwide survey of practices used in wooing the rain gods.

Of the things which the public magician sets himself to do for the good of the tribe [Frazer wrote], one of the chief is to control the weather and especially to ensure an adequate fall of rain.... Hence in savage communities the rain-maker is a very important personage; and often a special class of magicians exists for the purpose of regulating the heavenly water-supply. The methods by which they attempt to discharge the duties of their office are commonly, though not always, based on the principle of homeopathic or imitative magic. If they wish to make rain they simulate it by sprinkling water or mimicking clouds; if their object is to stop rain and cause drought, they avoid water and resort to warmth and fire for the sake of drying up the too abundant moisture.

A similar modern rain charm is "If you want it to rain, you pour out a bit of water on the ground."

Frazer cited scores of rainmaking methods used throughout the world. In New Guinea, for example, a wizard makes rain by dipping a branch of a particular kind of tree in water and then scattering the moisture from the dripping bough over the ground. A Javanese mode of making rain is to imitate the pattering sound of raindrops by brushing a coconut leaf over the sheath of a betel nut in a mortar. In Ceram, an island of Indonesia, it is considered enough to dedicate the bark of a certain tree to the spirits and place it in water. Every part of the world has its own unique method of rainmaking, and Frazer recounted them by the dozens.

Of all the forces of nature, lightning is perhaps the most feared. The Greeks and Romans, as well as primitive men, considered it evidence of the wrath of the gods. The Roman god Jupiter hurled lightning bolts when he became angry. In medieval days witches were thought to cause lightning.

In modern times a number of superstitions have developed, most of them dealing with means of protection against being struck by lightning. Some of the most popular are:

No one is killed by lightning when asleep. To be awakened by a streak of lightning when asleep is a fortunate omen.

If you wind a snake's skin around you, you cannot be struck.

It is unlucky to mention lightning immediately after the flash.

Whoever looks at lightning will become mad.

While a fire burns on the hearth, lightning will not strike a house.

A feather bed will keep lightning away.

The thorn tree is safe from lightning. A Sussex rhyme clarified this:

> Beware of the oak; it draws the stroke.
> Avoid the ash; it courts the flash.
> Creep under a thorn; it can save you from harm.

A common fear has always been that of being struck by lightning. This applies particularly to rural areas, where huge trees form excellent targets. Before the invention of lightning rods by Benjamin Franklin, farmers lived in the fear that their houses, barns, and haystacks would burn up, and so certain protective superstitions became popular:

Thunderstones (stones thought to have been broken from large bounders by thunder) placed at the front door are good charms against lightning.

Keeping a plant of live-forever (a hardy, long-lasting plant with purple flowers) will make a house safe.

A large bell should be rung at the approach of a storm.

From the most ancient days the Japanese have believed that a person under a mosquito net is safe from lightning.

Lightning forms in clouds that have become charged with electricity. During a storm this charge is attracted to the earth and concentrates on tall objects such as trees, chimneys, and church steeples. The electric attraction between a charged cloud and these objects on earth is greater than that between the clouds themselves. If this attraction becomes great enough, a huge electric spark may pass from the cloud to the earth. This spark, or flash of lightning, follows the path of least resistance, often varying its course at sharp angles. Therefore, high or isolated objects, especially if they are good conductors, are most often struck by lightning.

Some objects are more exposed to lightning than others. A tree on a hilltop or one standing in an open meadow is more exposed to lightning than one standing in a low place or in the midst of a number of trees. The largest number of fatalities occur on golf courses where players seek shelter under a large tree in an otherwise open area. Wire fences are also lightning attractors.

By its very nature as a holy place, a church was traditionally supposed to be safe, but the high steeples always attracted lightning. When this occurred, the devil was supposed to be taking vengeance upon Christians and the power of good over evil.

A widely quoted superstition is that "lightning never strikes twice in the same place." Although it is true that lightning doesn't usually strike in the same place, the idea that it could never occur is erroneous. The Empire State Building in New York City is also an effective lightning rod. The top is often struck by lightning, sometimes more than once, when a thunderstorm passes over Manhattan.

In fact, the Empire State Building has been struck as often as fifty times in just one summer.

By a freak of nature, even people have been struck twice. In Montrose, Colorado, in a 1948 summer storm, a young man was struck by lightning, staggered to his feet, and was struck again!

Thunder is the sound produced when a flash of lightning passes through the air, heating it and causing it to send out a sound wave, which is heard as the crash of thunder. The volume of its sound depends upon the amount of electricity discharged into the atmosphere. Primitive man interpreted this phenomenon as representing the anger of the gods. The most famous deities associated with the thunderbolt in ancient times were Zeus and Jupiter in Greek and Roman mythology, and their Norse counterpart, Thor. They are often pictured as hurling lightning bolts. Many people today continue to fear both lightning and thunder, a carry-over from the past.

Since thunder is now known to be harmless, few superstitions still exist concerning it. However, in connection with weather forecasting, a thunderstorm is invariably an indication of rain or, less often, snowstorms. In England and Wales, a winter thunderstorm is believed to foretell the death of a locally prominent man, and fierce storms are said to occur when a great man dies. Such a storm raged when Oliver Cromwell died (1658), and his enemies, the Royalists, asserted that it was caused by the devil, who had come to claim him.

10. Superstitions of the Sea

> "A great fear is the parent of superstition, but a discreet and well-guided fear produced religion."
> —Jeremy Taylor, English clergyman, *The Rule and Exercises of Holy Living* (1650)

Because of their perilous life and the mystery and uncertainty of the seas, sailors have always been particularly prone to belief in signs and omens. Since the time of Jonah they have been inclined to credit supernatural causes to perfectly natural phenomena and to be constantly alert for portents of troubles to come. In fact, a person or thing that was held to cause bad luck on a voyage came to be called a "Jonah." As James Fenimore Cooper commented,

SUPERSTITIONS OF THE SEA

There is a majesty in the might of the great deep that has a tendency to keep open the avenues of that dependent credulity which more or less besets the mind of every man. The confusion between things which are explicable and things which are not gradually brings the mind of the mariner to a state in which any exciting and unnatural sentiment is welcome.

In the days of sail the voyage of a ship and the welfare of the crew depended on the state of the weather. Imaginary dangers lurked everywhere and had to be overcome. Today the junks of Chinese sailors still have holes bored into the sails and rudders to allow evil spirits to slip through. Believing that a ship is blind, these sailors also paint eyes on the prow to aid in their voyages.

Of course, the average modern seaman is more secure, and the horrors of the deep make less of an impression on him. It is the old salts and the men of the less-than-modern freighters and tramp steamers that navigate the seven seas, often at the mercy of the elements, who are loath to surrender superstition to reality. Their traditional beliefs cover almost every aspect of the sailor's life, centering on both the ship itself and its encounters with the elements.

Even today the ceremony associated with the launching of a ship is surrounded by superstition. In distant times, particularly among the Vikings, blood from human beings or animals was spread on the prow, as a tribute to the sea spirits, in the belief that life would be given to the ship and the crew protected.

The Greeks and Romans were the first to spatter their triremes and warcraft with offerings of red wine to win the protection of the gods. These offerings were made in the

Some years ago an English shipowner, finding that none of his vessels could get off to sea on Friday, owing to the feeling among the sailors, determined to cure the madness if he could. He therefore laid the keel of a vessel on Friday, made every contract concerning the construction on Friday, and launched the craft on the unlucky day. He christened the ship with this name, and found an old sea captain called Friday whom he made master for her first voyage. She was loaded for an East India port, and after great difficulty in securing a crew she sailed on a given Friday for her destination. She was never spoken of or heard from after the pilot left her. The presumption is that when she encountered her first storm, the sailors, who are proverbially superstitious, became apprehensive and took to the boats, leaving the ill-fated craft to founder in midocean and to perish themselves in like manner.

The account ended with the comment:

It is singular how one such incident will deepen a prejudice already existing and establish in the minds of many, who are otherwise sensible, a connection between two events that can have no possible relation to each other.

Even the British Royal Navy observed this taboo. During World War I, when a ceaseless stream of new ships was vital, there was no known instance of a Friday launching. A story often repeated, though no ship named *Friday* has been registered in the twentieth century, is that the Admiralty, to disprove the superstition, laid the keel of a ship on Friday, launched her on Friday, and embarked her on her first voyage on a Friday. The vessel proved completely unseaworthy!

The adoption of modern mechanical methods for loading and unloading has reduced the time a vessel spends in port, resulting in very crowded time schedules, and the notion of detaining a ship for a whole day in deference to a superstition has become too ridiculous even to consider. Hence the belief is no longer generally observed.

Other beliefs concerning bad and good luck, however, have persisted and are still believed. Shipowners will rarely purchase a vessel that has a history of disaster; bad luck is said to pursue certain ships, leading to their reputations as being jinxed. Carrying dead bodies brings disaster, and was said to be one of the reasons for the burial of crew members at sea, although the lack of refrigeration on many ships seems a more plausible explanation for this.

On the other hand, some sailors believe that a sick man on board ship will not die until land has been sighted. One of the superstitions firmly believed in the days of sail and of whaling ships was that sharks knew when death was coming and would follow such a ship for miles, waiting for the moment when the dead body, wrapped in a sheet, would be thrown into the sea. A persistently following shark was therefore held to be a certain death omen, and the fact that one was following was usually concealed from any sick person. As far as is known, however, this superstition has no foundation in fact. Sharks follow in the wake of vessels for the same reason that all fish do, solely for the scraps of meat and food that are thrown overboard.

An odd belief in the past was that if one struck a glass

or a bowl and allowed it to ring, without stopping the vibration with the hand, it would surely result in the death of a crew member by drowning. The saying was "Ring a glass and drown a sailor." Another act that was considered highly unlucky was to drink the health of any person in water, for this resulted in a curse, as though expressing a wish that the individual so toasted might drown.

There is a miscellany of superstitions regarding the sea. It is unlucky to have an umbrella on a vessel; also, no one carrying a black suitcase should be allowed on board. It is unlucky to drive nails on Sunday. If one watches a ship out of sight, it may never be seen again, or misfortune will come to the vessel whether it contains anyone known to the watcher or not. A variation is that pointing at a ship at sea or leaving the harbor will bring bad luck to those on board and may cause a shipwreck.

The rat figures in two superstitions. Watch for rats before putting out to sea, for if they leave, the ship will be lost. The proverbial desertion of sinking ships by rats is founded upon reason and undoubtedly occurs. Rats will stay in one place so long as food is plentiful, but they hate to be wet, so it is probable that the ship they leave is leaky and unseaworthy.

A cat is welcome on board ship because it brings luck, especially if it is entirely black (a complete reversal of the unlucky-black-cat superstition). Undoubtedly, cats were useful in catching rats, too. However, one belief had it that a black cat "carried a gale in her tail," and if she became unusually frisky and playful, a storm was sure to follow.

Much of the lore of seamen concerns omens that forecast the weather, an all-important matter in their lives. The English author Thomas Gibbons, in an account of the life of seamen in the days of sail titled *Boxing the Compass,* explained this preoccupation. "There is but a plank between a sailor and eternity," he wrote, "and perhaps the occasional realization of that fact may have had something to do with the broad grain of superstition at one time undoubtedly lurking in his nature."

One of the most widely accepted weather superstitions concerns whistling at sea, called whistling for the wind. Seamen generally consider it extremely unlucky because to whistle is to imitate the wind, and so may cause a storm. In a calm a soft whistle produces a breeze, but if it is too loud, an undesirable gale will result. A fair wind may also be produced, a superstition tells us, if a pack of playing cards is thrown overboard. If a sailor sneezes on the port side, the voyage will prove unlucky; if on the starboard, favorable winds can be expected.

For centuries sailors have believed that some seabirds, notably gulls and petrels, were creatures of ill omen, chiefly because they were thought to be the souls of dead sailors wandering aimlessly in the sky and following the ships for long periods. However, they should never be killed. The huge albatross, the largest seabird, has a wingspread of from ten to twelve feet, but its wings, which are very long, measure only about nine inches in width. It can remain aloft in midocean for long periods. Even though the bird brings winds and fogs, which are not always welcome, it, like the other incarnations of sailors' spirits, should never be killed.

The latter prohibition formed the basis of Samuel Taylor Coleridge's world-famous poem, *The Rime of the Ancient Mariner,* first published in 1798, when albatrosses were frequently encountered at sea. The ship became becalmed for a long period, and the old sailor who had killed the albatross was inconsolable:

> And I had done a hellish thing,
> And it would work 'em woe.
> For all averred, I had killed the bird
> That made the breeze to blow.
> Ah wretch! said they, the bird to slay,
> That made the breeze to blow!

The dead bird was hung around his neck as a punishment. Though Coleridge admitted that the poem was entirely a work of the imagination, the legend he created has been perpetuated; all reference books cite this as the source of the superstition against killing the albatross.

When no moon is visible during a ship's ordinary passage, storms will follow. Henry Wadsworth Longfellow employed this belief in *The Wreck of the Hesperus:*

> For I fear a hurricane.
> Last night, the moon had a golden ring,
> And tonight no moon we see!

The lore of seamen is filled with strange tales. In complete seriousness they have accepted stories of mermaids and sea serpents, the truth of which has often been sworn to. However, stories concerning phantom or ghost ships are even more numerous, the most famous being that of the Flying Dutchman. This tale is told with variations in every maritime country, differing each time only in details.

The accepted version tells of a Dutch captain who had vainly tried to round Cape Horn (the Cape of Good Hope in some versions) in a terrific gale. The rounding of Cape Horn was always mentioned in accounts of early round-the-world navigators because of the rough weather there. The captain swore that he would accomplish the feat, and when the gale increased, he laughed at the fears of his crew, even throwing overboard several members who threatened to mutiny. The Holy Ghost appeared near the ship in the tempest, but in firing his pistol at the apparition, the Dutchman pierced his own hand and paralyzed his arm. For that, he cursed God, and because of his blasphemy he was condemned to wander endlessly until the Day of Judgment, without ever putting into port, and to have only gall (bile) to drink, red-hot iron to eat, and a watch to keep that would last forever. His crew suffered with him.

The Dutchman became an evil omen to all. Anyone who saw him would suffer ill fortune, and in his anger he would send storms, disasters, and gales. Wine would sour and food become rancid. In keeping with the tradition, many memoirs tell of seeing him as they rounded the Cape and of being followed by desperate trials.

The sight of what is called Saint Elmo's fire is more explicable. The name was taken from that of Erasmus, patron saint of Mediterranean seamen, who was said to have died at sea during a severe storm. In his last moments he promised to return and show himself to the crew in some form if they survived the storm. Soon after his death a strange light appeared at the masthead; it was assumed to be the saint himself, or fire sent by him, in fulfillment of his promise to watch over the crew.

Saint Elmo's fire is actually a natural phenomenon. Frequently, a bright, glowing light appears in the masts of ships, which is caused by electric discharges during storms. It can also be seen today around airplanes flying through charged clouds and sometimes in mountain regions when thunderstorms are passing over high peaks. Its appearance is startling at first sight, for the objects it touches seem to be enveloped in it, and it is often accompanied by a crackling noise like the sound of twigs or dry grass burning.

Because the light generally appears when the worst of a storm is over, sailors have always welcomed it and considered it a fortunate sign. Christopher Columbus cheered his restless and almost mutinous crew on the voyage to America by pointing to the glow at the masthead and predicting an early end to their troubles. In his journals, Ferdinand Magellan also mentions the feeling of comfort and hope he experienced from these lights of Saint Elmo in times of danger. The spectacle is mentioned in Richard Henry Dana's classic *Two Years Before the Mast,* and in Herman Melville's novel *Moby Dick.*

11. Folk Medicine

> "Sickness and sorrows come and go,
> but a superstitious soul hath no rest."
> —Robert Burton, English clergyman,
> *The Anatomy of Melancholy* (1621)

The history of medicine, to quote H. Stanley Redgrove, an authority on ancient magic and mysticism, "is at once the history of human wisdom and the history of human credulity and folly."

Until comparatively recent times, in view of the long history of the healing art, magic and medicine were closely allied. It might correctly be stated that medicine was a specialized branch of the art of magic, for magic covered every phase of human activity and thought.

The use of herbs as medicines, though dating back to ancient times, began in Europe in the fifteenth century.

Some of the first books printed in movable type were botanical treatises in Latin, English, and German, filled with queer superstitions about the healing properties of plants and with prayers and incantations to be recited when using them for medicinal purposes. Many plants are used in modern drugs, such as digitalis, the dried leaf of the foxglove.

The road to the present was paved with dangerous practices and with trial and error. Even now, with medicine at the stage where it is almost entirely free of blindly accepted and unproved beliefs, the ignorant and credulous continue to hold to their own notions. Incredible as it may seem, many people still use magic to cure illness or to ward off disease. Folk medicine abounds, and it is practiced by individuals who apparently have more faith in their own home remedies than in doctors.

One of the best-selling books published in the United States in 1958 was *Folk Medicine: A Vermont Doctor's Guide to Good Health,* which was written by D. C. Jarvis, an experienced country doctor. Dr. Jarvis suggested treating such common ailments as colds and fevers and aches and pains with easy everyday remedies like honey, apple cider, castor oil, and corn oil rather than with recognized medicines that a more modern physician would prescribe. This book sold three million copies.

The popular folk beliefs listed below are typical of the thousands that are rampant:

It is dangerous to sleep in the moonlight, because the moon controls lunacy, and to let its rays fall on the pillow will turn you into an idiot.

The best way to get a cinder out of your eye is to rub the other eye. Another way is to blow your nose on the side concerned.

Treat a headache by pressing the roof of your mouth with your thumb.

In Indiana and in various other civilized states, a madstone, a stony mass such as a hair ball taken from the stomach of a deer, is sometimes used to cure hydrophobia.

An expectant mother must eat enough for two.

The idea that the expectant mother can influence her child is one of the most common of all impressions. Hence mothers desiring handsome or artistic children visit the art institutes, and those wishing a Van Cliburn keep the neighbors awake by playing the piano.

In Arizona it is still generally believed that the drinking of two quarts of whiskey will cure snakebite.

There are all sorts of techniques for curing warts, the favorite method being to tie as many knots in a string as there are warts to be removed; then the string is buried by the light of the moon at a crossroads. The first person who passes gets the warts.

Everyone has a special formula for curing or preventing a cold. These include the hot toddy, soaking the feet in hot water, wearing light underwear all the year round, taking a cold bath every morning, and starvation.

There are innumerable cures for hiccups, one of the most common being to count slowly up to one hundred.

This list of prevailing and accepted beliefs could be even longer. The majority of such beliefs have not the slightest basis in fact, and most represent the simplest form of autosuggestion, turning the mind away from the symptom to something else, or are an attempt to transfer the trouble to somebody or something else.

Superstitions and fallacies are most prevalent where people cannot obtain medical aid and have to rely on the doctoring advice of those around them. Sometimes the treatment is based on common sense; other times the neighborhood advice is full of traditional lore, and remedies are suggested that have been used for many generations with varying degrees of success. As Dr. H. W. Haggard of Yale University commented, "Most people secretly believe in the occasional accomplishment of the impossible, and secretly believe that scientists who scoff at their beliefs are wrong."

In spite of increased government supervision, quacks, who promise miraculous and immediate cures, do a flourishing business. Millions of dollars are spent in the United States for patent medicines. An individual using them may get over his illness, but his recovery is probably due to the natural resistance of his body to disease.

Folk medicine abounds with protective charms and amulets that are worn around the neck or placed on the affected area—a backward step toward the taboos, magic practices, and voodoo rites of the past. The hearing of many a child has been damaged because a mother has allowed running ears to go uncared for, believing that it is a good omen to have the poison leave his system. "It's the mischief coming out," she will say. American Southerners in the red-clay section of Alabama make a poultice of the clay with vinegar for sprains—elsewhere this may be made with cow manure. The hot blood of a chicken is a "sure cure" for snakebite, as contrasted with the universal folk remedy, whiskey, which does nothing more than take the mind of the bitten person off his discomfort. Some people believe the swelling from a beesting will subside if a wad of chewed tobacco is applied.

In almost every country in the world, bags of fetid material are considered to be effective in warding off disease. Italians favor garlic, but asafetida, with its nauseous odor, is the most popular among those who wear such bags. The belief is that the sickening odor will keep people with contagious diseases at a distance, but it does not protect against people with colds, who have temporarily lost their sense of smell!

"Feed a cold and starve a fever" is the slogan for an old, commonly accepted folklore remedy. A person with a cold is encouraged to eat an abundance of food to build up his resistance, but to take in little food when fever is a symptom. According to modern knowledge, this old adage is completely wrong. Most physicians treat colds by cutting down on food and increasing liquids.

The methods of treating colds through folk medicine are many. For example, teas brewed with leaves of all sorts are used as medicine. A British country belief is that peeled onions attract germs, and a cold will move from the patient to them. The onions are placed in a sickroom so the cold will "go away."

In many American homes people still treat the common cold by padding the chest with layers of absorbent cotton soaked in camphor and goose grease. There are also many widely advertised liniments for chest colds, the application of which is supposed to draw off infection. In folk medicine whiskey is a miracle worker and should be taken in great quantities. Sweating is a part of all treatments.

Rheumatism and arthritis are accompanied by severe, nagging pains. So many people suffer from the latter disease that a great deal of research is being conducted on it. During the decade of the 1960's over two dozen books for general readers were published about arthritis, the most popular being *Arthritis and Folk Medicine,* the second book of the Vermont country doctor. Its suggestions of simple home remedies attracted millions of sufferers, who purchased the paperback editions of the book.

For several years a recommended cure for both rheumatism and arthritis was the wearing of a copper wire around the waist or as a bracelet, the combination of metal and flesh supposedly creating electricity, which would bring relief. In the late 1960's the wires were sold in large numbers in spite of the much publicized opinions of doctors and specialists that they were completely ineffective. This is an excellent example of medical quackery appealing to sufferers who hope to find relief from pain.

Anything resembling an eye has always been thought to have magic in it. That may be why many Americans carry a horse chestnut, or buckeye, in the pocket as a way to fend off pain. For the same reason, people in some parts of Britain carry a potato. The potato should be a new one, and it should be kept until it has turned black and is as hard as old wood. The belief that it is a cure for pains in the joints is shared by both country and city people.

One of the continuously popular remedies for rheumatism or arthritis is to wear red flannel over the afflicted part. Because it is the color of blood, red symbolizes life and circulation and is thought to have great value.

Before the development of modern dentistry, a toothache, too, was cured by charms. During the Middle Ages more than twenty saints were supposed to have the power to relieve or cure it. Some of the folk remedies that still survive are pathetically ridiculous—for example, "Tying a string around the small toe on the right foot will stop a toothache on the left side of the jaw," or vice versa. That various herbal teas and mixtures can kill toothache pain is also patently untrue.

Warts have bedeviled man for thousands of years, and dermatologists have yet to discover the reason or the remedy for them, although they do think they are caused by a virus. According to a twenty-year study made by an Ohio dermatologist and reported in a 1971 issue of *Time*, warts are contagious. He found that 60 percent of all warts are spread between family members and urges people with warts to keep them covered. When necessary, most doctors remove warts by medically proved methods such as burning, freezing, and cauterizing. But laymen have been equally successful with an assortment of home remedies, some of which, astounding as it seems, are approved by doctors.

Treatments for the removal of warts form a substantial body of folklore. Rubbing certain kinds of juices on them is the most popular, and scores of rites are recorded. Typical of these rites is that if you hold a knotted string over the wart and then bury the string, the wart will disappear, an act smacking of exorcism. It is similar to the act of spitting on a piece of string that has touched the wart and keeping it; when the string rots, the wart drops off. The belief that warts are caused by handling toads, though untrue, is widespread; this belief may have originated because of the wartlike appearance of the toad's skin.

There is documentary evidence that warts have disappeared after being touched with a copper penny or a slice of raw potato. However, warts often disappear for no apparent reason, and whatever may have been done to them beforehand usually receives the credit. Some sufferers insist that they have found relief in Tom Sawyer's prescription for "spunk water" (rain from a tree stump in the woods). Still others have employed the services of old women in the hills of eastern Kentucky, who are said to cure warts by merely touching them.

An attack of the hiccups (or hiccoughs), although usually harmless, can be a most annoying and uncomfortable experience. Often painful and persistent, an attack is particularly distressing because there is no reliable way to stop it. Hiccups become serious only when they continue for a long period, wearing down the vitality of the sufferer, who can neither sleep nor eat properly.

Home remedies in folk medicine have been abundant. The most familiar one is to frighten the person with the hiccups. Slowly sipping water or drinking water around a pencil (the German version is to take a long draft of beer from a mug with a bare knife in it), standing on one's head, holding the nose as long as possible without taking a breath, and breathing into a paper bag have been established remedies, though not always successful.

One of the oldest folk treatments has been swallowing a spoonful of sugar. In the past doctors gave it no more credence than any of the other popular cures. However, this remedy was never subjected to controlled tests until 1971, when Dr. Edgar Engleman, of the University of California School of Medicine, proved its efficacy.

Dr. Engleman's wife suffered a severe attack of hiccups at a party, and one of the guests suggested that she take some sugar. She did, and the hiccups stopped almost immediately.

Dr. Engleman decided to try out the cure on a larger number of subjects. Out of twenty sufferers, twelve had had the hiccups for less than six hours when they sought treatment. The remaining eight had been afflicted with persistent hiccups for twenty-four hours to six weeks. Five had tried tranquilizers and the old folk remedies, all without success.

One teaspoonful of ordinary white granulated sugar swallowed dry proved immediately successful in most cases, and the few who suffered renewed attacks responded to the same treatment. Dr. Engleman's explanation is that the sugar granules apparently irritated the nerve endings in the back of the throat and interfered with the nerve impulses causing the hiccups. In this instance, then, the folk remedy was effective, an indication that whoever first used it had come up with a cure with no apparent medical knowledge.

12. Love and Courtship

> "He loves me, he loves me not...."
> —Daisy petal ritual

There are many superstitions that uniquely concern youthful love with all its vagaries and uncertainties. Most of them are meant to help a girl find a sweetheart and eventually a husband. Since young men seem to be more practical and less sentimental, few superstitions pertain to them.

The greatest number of rituals and sayings involving love are local ones, and this chapter will deal with superstitions common to the English-speaking world. Nearly all have their origins in the past. Folklore abounds with love charms in the form of rhymes and spells, talismans and potions. To moderns they may seem completely ridiculous, but they are still practiced in rural areas.

In the north of England, for example, a girl before going to bed might place her shoes in the form of a T, saying,

> Hoping this night my true love to see,
> I place my shoes in the form of a T.

American Southerners believe that if a girl holds a mirror over a well, she will see the image of her future husband. Also, if a girl puts a looking glass under her pillow, she will dream of her lover.

A supposedly effective action is for a girl to plant an onion or any bulb in a new pot while saying the name of the one she loves. Each morning and evening thereafter, she repeats this rhyme:

> As this root grows,
> As this blossom blows,
> May his heart be
> Turned unto me.

Another rhyme is to be spoken by a girl who has picked two long-stemmed roses and names one for herself and one for the boy she wishes to attract. Kneeling beside her bed, she focuses her eyes on the rose named for her lover, twines the stems of both roses together, and repeats this verse:

> Twine, twine and intertwine,
> Let my love be wholly mine;

> If his heart be kind and true,
> Deeper grow his rose's hue.

If her lover is to succumb, the color of his rose will grow darker.

In England several of the saints' days are considered particularly favorable for maidens. The night of January 20, called Saint Agnes' Eve, is still superstitiously regarded as a time when a girl who performs certain rites may see the image of her future husband. In northeast England these rites have to be preceded by a rigid fast lasting the whole day. No food, drink, or speech are permitted. John Keats's familiar poem, "The Eve of St. Agnes," describes the ceremony:

> They told me how, upon St. Agnes' Eve,
> Young virgins might have visions of delight,
> And soft adorings from their loves receive
> Upon the honeyed middle of the night,
> If ceremonies due they did aright;
> As, supperless to bed they must retire,
> And couch supine their beauties, lily white,
> Nor look behind, nor sideways, but require
> Of heaven with upward eyes for all that they
>   desire.

One Saint Agnes' Eve spell directed a girl to take a row of pins stuck on paper and pull out every one, one after another, saying a Paternoster. Then she was to stick them in a row on one sleeve of her nightgown.

Another love spell involved knots, which always symbolize ties of various sorts. The ceremony is described as follows: Knit the left garter about the right-legged stocking, and as you recite this verse, at every comma knit a knot:

> This knot I knit,
> To know the thing I know not yet,
> That I may see
> The man that shall my husband be.

Another dream charm for January 20 said to take a sprig of rosemary, a magic plant in popular tradition, and another of thyme, sprinkle them three times with water, place one in each shoe, and then place a shoe with the sprig in it on each side of the bed, repeating,

> Saint Agnes, that's to lovers kind,
> Come ease the trouble of my mind.

Scottish lasses sow grain at midnight, saying,

> Agnes sweet and Agnes fair,
> Hither, hither now repair.
> Bonnie Agnes, let me see
> The lad who is to marry me.

The figure of the future sweetheart is supposed to appear to the girl as if reaping the grain.

Two other English religious days are propitious for "seeing" the man of a girl's dream. Making a "dumb cake" was a well-known rural charm to induce a vision, or dream, of the maker's future husband. Complete silence was to be maintained throughout the rite, hence the name. It was thought to be particularly effective on October 6, Saint Faith's Day, though it might also be undertaken on Saint Agnes' Eve. A cake was made of flour, water, eggs, and salt, sometimes by several young people together. The finished cake was divided equally, and immediately afterward, while observing complete silence, each girl walked backward upstairs to her bedroom, where she ate her portion before getting into bed. During the night she would dream of her future husband. This ritual varied in different sections of the country. It could also be performed by young men who wanted to see their future brides.

Hoping to determine whether or not they would be married when they grew up and to discover a clue to their future mate's name, English country girls and boys were directed to peel an apple in one continous piece. The peeling was then to be thrown over the left shoulder to discover whether or not they would eventually be married. If the peel broke, the thrower would never marry; if it remained unbroken, marriage was ensured, and the shape of the peeling on the ground indicated the initial letter of the future partner.

To determine if she will find a lover or be married, an American girl of marriageable age might count the seeds of an apple, with the formula:

> One, I love, two, I love,
> Three, I love, I say;
> Four, I love with all my heart,
> And five I cast away.
> Six, he loves me,
> Seven, she loves,
> Eight, they both love.
> Nine, he comes,

Ten, he tarries,
Eleven, he courts,
Twelve, he marries.

The universally observed day of lovers is February 14, Saint Valentine's Day. On that day millions of cards are sent to persons of the opposite sex. Formerly, the cards were individually made and love rhymes or sentiments written on them.

In ancient Rome the date honored the goddess Juno, and in Greece, Hera, the guardian of women and marriage. The early Christian Church appropriated the date, linking it with the martyrdom of Saint Valentine, a young priest. Saint Valentine had defied the edict of Emperor Claudius, which abolished marriage because husbands did not make good soldiers, and performed the marriage ceremony for young lovers. For this he was imprisoned and killed on February 14, 269, and he became the patron saint of lovers.

In England the custom of sending messages to one's beloved on Saint Valentine's Day began during the Middle Ages. In later times the strict rules of love and courtship were abandoned on this date.

A belief held in both Britain and the United States holds that an eligible girl can foretell her future husband's position in life by the kind of birds she sees on Saint Valentine's Day.

A blackbird: a clergyman
A redbreast or bunting: a sailor
A goldfinch: a millionaire
A yellowbird: a rich man
A sparrow: love in a cottage

A bluebird: poverty [in modern times the bluebird has come to be a symbol of happiness]
A crossbill: a quarrelsome husband
A flock of doves: good luck
A wryneck [woodpecker]: she will never marry.

Some Saint Valentine's Day beliefs are:

If a girl peeps through the keyhole on Saint Valentine's Day and sees a rooster and hen together, it is a sign that she will be married before the year is over.

If a girl looks out into the street the first thing in the morning, the number of animals she sees will tell her just how many years it will be before she is married.

On Saint Valentine's Day one should wear a yellow crocus; it is the saint's special flower and will ward off all evil in love.

If you chance to see a goldfinch or any yellowbird, it is extremely lucky.

The first young man or girl you meet will be your future husband or wife.

A superstition that is disregarded more often than not states that a valentine card should never be signed with one's own name, for it will not be successful. If a girl receives an unsigned valentine and wishes to find out who sent it, she should write her name on the back of it with the names of the persons she thinks might have sent it below. She should then repeat this rhyme:

> If he who sent this valentine
> Is named above with mine,
> I pray, good saint, that by this line
> I may his name divine.

Unfortunately, Saint Valentine's Day has become commercialized, and much of its traditional significance has been lost.

An essential part of courting is spooning, which derived from a Welsh custom. Before the Welsh used engagement rings, a young man used to carve a wooden spoon with elaborate lovers' knots and initials, suitably intertwined, and present it as a token of love to the girl of his choice. If she accepted it, it was as good as a promise of marriage. Spooning came to mean a show of affection, such as kissing and hugging.

Indeed, since ancient times kissing has been a way to show affection. Some anthropologists claim that the kiss developed because primitive man believed that the air he breathed possessed a magic power: He thought that when men and women kissed each other, they mingled their souls. According to British superstition, if a dark-complexioned man kisses a girl, she may expect a proposal from him. But, alas, if a girl kisses a man and gets a hair from his moustache on her lips, she will die an old maid!

If a girl wishes to see an absent lover, she should, according to a British superstition, pick the first flower she sees, breathe on it, and say, "Flower pink, flower white, I wish to see my love tonight!" Her true love will be sure to come, but he may not be the one she is thinking of. Candles may also be used to bring her lover to her side. A local British superstition holds that a girl can call her beloved by putting two pins into a lighted candle and reciting this verse:

> 'Tis not these pins I wish to burn,
> But —— 's heart I wish to turn.
> May he neither sleep nor rest
> 'Til he has granted my request.

Absent lovers have always written to each other, and such letters have often represented the finest examples of composition. But superstitions surround such correspondence:

If your hand trembles as you write to your beloved, his love for you is strong.

To make a blot on a love letter shows that the person you are writing to is thinking of you at the moment.

If you make a wish while writing a letter to your sweetheart under an oak tree, your wish will come true.

If a girl is reading her first love letter and the clock strikes twelve, the man who wrote it will never marry her.

If a girl receives two letters from two different suitors at the same time, she will never marry either of them.

If a man writes a love letter to a girl in pencil, it is a sign that they will never marry.

Never send a typewritten love letter unless you and your lover completely understand each other, so that it will make no difference; otherwise the reply will not be pleasant.

Never ask your lover a favor on a postal card; it will bring an unsatisfactory reply.

Don't mail a love letter on Sunday, or you will have a dispute with your lover.

A love letter insufficiently stamped is an evil sign.

If your lover sends you an unsealed letter, it is a sign that he is growing cold toward you.

To find out if your lover is true, set fire to one of his letters. If the flame is high and clear, his love is true, but if it is small and blue, he will forsake you.

If you keep a love letter in your shoe, your lover will be faithful to you.

To burn letters from a sweetheart is very bad luck; they should be torn up.

A good many beliefs are involved in the process of proposing:

To marry after a very brief acquaintance will not prove lucky; a year of courtship and three months of engagement are lucky.

A long courtship and a long engagement are usually, in the end, unlucky.

If a young lady is so surprised as to scream when unexpectedly approached by her lover, she will accept him if he proposes.

If, when proposing, a young man is interrupted by another young girl, she will one day become his second wife.

Much unexpected luck will follow if you receive a proposal of marriage at a dance but do not accept it.

It is a bad omen to receive a proposal of marriage on a train or bus or in any public place.

The man who has been refused three times should never ask again, as he would be happier unmarried.

An engagement by mail will be unlucky.

If many objections are made to a girl's marriage, it forebodes trouble for her.

If the love is of the once-in-a-lifetime variety, or, unhappy thought, if a desperate girl fears that she will become an old maid, she may take action to receive a proposal and become engaged to be married. A girl about to take such a step should beware, however, for it is said:

> The maid who asks a man to wed
> Will come to want and beg for bread.

The tradition of sealing the engagement with a ring has its origin in ancient times, when a ring was used as a pledge in any important agreement. The diamond ring is traditional and still popular. An ancient superstition held that the sparkle of the diamond originated in the alchemic fires of love, the spark of emotional love.

According to British belief, the day on which the man buys the ring is important and foretells the future:

On Monday: You will have a bustling life, full of excitement.

On Tuesday: You will have an easy life, contented and free.

On Wednesday: Your partner will be gay and good-natured.

Thursday: You will gain what you desire.

Friday: You will work hard, but the results will be good.

Saturday: You will always have cause to rejoice.

It is interesting to note that the future always promises happiness. However, if the bride buys the ring, she will never live happily with her husband.

It is considered unlucky to alter the first width of an engagement ring; instead it should be exchanged. If the ring wears down and becomes loose before the marriage, it is wiser not to marry, since only disaster will follow. If the lover drops the ring while trying to put it on the girl's finger, the couple will never wed. It is also unlucky to lose an engagement ring.

Finally, the lapse of time before the marriage will take place can be determined through charms and omens:

If an engaged girl stumbles over a bottle, she will not be married for a year.

Dip a feather in water, and the number of drops that fall from it after you shake it will be the number of years before you are married.

To find out how many years it will be before you are married, you should fill a glass tumbler two-thirds full of water, pull a hair out of your head, and tie it to a thimble. Taking the other end of the hair between your thumb and finger, suspend the thimble over the center of the glass, and say the following words:

> As many years as I live single, -
> Let this thimble knock and jingle.

With true love triumphant after the courtship and engagement, the bond between the lovers will be sealed in the marriage ceremony.

14. Marriage

> "Where there's marriage without love,
> there will be love without marriage."
> —Benjamin Franklin, *Poor Richard's Almanac* (1734)

Marriage is admittedly one of life's highlights, and the variety of superstitions, local and universal, concerning weddings is almost endless. Because the rite dates back to primitive times, many modern beliefs have their origins in ancient practices.

The planning of all elements in a wedding involves precautions that must be taken so that good luck and happiness will result. The first item to be settled, of course, is the time—the month and day. To the superstitious, this matter is not as easy to decide as it would seem.

MARRIAGE

A prospective British bride may be aided in her decision regarding the month by the rhyme:

> Married in January's hoar and rime
> Widowed you'll be before your prime.
> Married in February's sleepy weather
> Life you'll tread in time together.
> Married when March winds shrill and roar
> Your home will be on a distant shore.
> Married 'neath April's changeful skies
> A checquered path before you lies.
> Married when bees o'er May blossoms flit
> Strangers around your board will sit.
> Married in month of roses—June
> Life will be one long honeymoon.
> Married in July with flowers ablaze
> Bitter-sweet memories on after days.
> Married in August's heat and drowse
> Lover and friend in your chosen spouse.
> Married in September's golden glow
> Smooth and serene your life will go.
> Married when leaves in October thin
> Toil and hardship for you begin.
> Married in veils of November mist
> Fortune your wedding ring has kissed.
> Married in days of December cheer
> Love's star shines brighter from year to year.

The popular notion that June is the luckiest time of the year appears to have originated among the ancient Romans. June was named after the goddess Juno, good and faithful wife of Jupiter. She was regarded as the goddess of youth and of marriage and was the protector of women.

Her blessing and protection followed all those wedded in her month.

More practically, June is desirable because of its weather, but although May is also one of the brightest months in the year, it is considered to be very unlucky—in fact, the worst month that can be chosen for a wedding. This belief is also of Roman origin. May was named after the goddess Maia, wife of Vulcan, god of fire. In addition to being the goddess of fertility, she was the patroness of the aged, and the month is therefore avoided by young lovers. The Roman poet Ovid wrote:

> Let maid or widow that would turn a wife,
> Avoid the scorn that's dangerous to life!
> If you will mind old saws, mind this: I say
> 'Tis bad to marry in the month of May.

To the Catholic bride-to-be, May is the month of the Virgin Mary. Scots have believed that because the ill-fated Queen Mary married Lord Bothwell in May and the alliance proved disastrous, evil would come to all who wedded in that month.

The wedding day may be selected from several contradictory British lists, two of which are:

Married on Sunday . . . a happy future.
Married on Monday, you will be enriched by a foreigner.
Married on Tuesday brings great benefit to the children of the union.
Married on Wednesday . . . an event of great consequence will occur within a month.
Married on Thursday, you will have several children.

Married on Friday . . . a strange home within a year.
Married on Saturday . . . foretells an enviable fate.

or:

> Wed on Monday, always poor;
> Wed on Tuesday, wed once more;
> Wed on Wednesday, happy match;
> Wed on Thursday, splendid catch;
> Wed on Friday, poorly mated;
> Wed on Saturday, better waited;
> Wed on Sunday, Cupid's wooing;
> In the morning, quick undoing.

Considered solely on the basis of the good or bad luck that may result, an American Negro superstition advises the future bride:

> Monday: a bad day.
> Tuesday: a good day. You will have a good husband and live long.
> Wednesday: a fine day. You will have an excellent husband, will live happily in spite of some trouble.
> Thursday: a bad day.
> Friday: a bad day.
> Saturday: no luck at all.
> Sunday: no luck at all.

In summary, Wednesday appears to be the most favorable day, Friday unlucky, and Saturday the unluckiest. Evidently, thousands of modern brides refuse to accept the belief regarding Saturday, because that is the day most often chosen for a wedding. It is undoubtedly due to the fact that Saturday is the day when most people are free from work.

For some unexplained reason, there is an old superstition that it is unlucky to be married on one's birthday.

Once the date has been set, however, postponement of the wedding should be avoided, for every sort of conceivable bad luck is sure to result.

One of the persistent worries of the wedding planner is that the weather will be unfavorable on the happy day. All future brides recall the old sayings "Happy is the bride the sun shines on" and its opposite, "Unhappy is the bride the rain falls on." One reason for these beliefs lies in the fact that all early British ceremonies took place in the open air, generally at the church door and not inside the building. Since raindrops symbolize tears, an American belief holds that if it rains on the wedding, the bride will cry all during her married life. Storms portend great unhappiness and grief, but snow, apparently because of its pure white, the color the bride is dressed in, is looked upon as a good sign.

The making of the wedding dress is surrounded by traditional beliefs and rules, many of which are still very much alive today. Although every item of the bride's clothing will probably be new, there are two exceptions, the "old" and "borrowed" items in the universally accepted saying:

> Something old, something new,
> Something borrowed, something blue.

Traditionally, the bride is dressed in all white—except for "something blue"—which indicates that she is a virgin and innocent. Colors are usually used in the gowns of the

MARRIAGE

bride's attendants. It is considered lucky if a mother gives her white bridal dress to the first of her daughters to be married, and in some ancestry-minded families, a gown may be worn by one or more descendant brides. Widows and divorcées, of course, do not wear white; even an off-white or flesh color is considered to be in bad taste.

An English rhyme describes the symbolism of the various possible colors:

> Married in white, you have chosen aright;
> Married in red, you'd sooner be dead;
> Married in yellow, ashamed of the fellow;
> Married in blue, your lover is true;
> Married in green, ashamed to be seen;
> Married in black, you'll ride in a hack [hearse];
> Married in pearl, you'll live in a whirl;
> Married in pink, your spirits will sink;
> Married in brown, you'll live out of town.

These negative and positive results appear to have been devised for purposes of rhyme. Some colors, however, possess a significance of their own.

The luckiest shades are considered to be blue, pink, and gold. Red brings very bad luck, and a drop of blood on a white dress, even if it is from a pinprick and the stain has been removed, means that the bride will not live long. Purple, a combination of red and blue, is considered inappropriate; in Japan, wearing it means that love will soon fade. Blue is popular because it represents love and constancy.

Because it represents jealousy (the "green-eyed monster"), green brings unhappiness. It has always been considered an unlucky color, connected with bad fairies, and among the English and Scots it foretells a change into mourning clothes. In Lowland Scotland, it was once thought so ill-omened that not only the bride but also the wedding guests were forbidden to wear it, and nothing green was permitted in the decorations. On the other hand, green is also the color of hope, so a bride can take a chance if she wishes.

Black, the color of mourning, is avoided, of course, or the bride will suffer all sorts of misfortunes and endure much sorrow in her new life. Fawn, a light grayish brown, for some inexplicable reason, means that the bride will cross the ocean at least once. Bridal gowns should be all-white or all one color; figures designs in the fabric are taboo. A vinelike pattern signifies death, and birds are a bad omen.

Silk, or a variation such as moiré, is the conventional white material. For reasons never clarified, satin is unlucky, and velvet is thought to bring poverty.

It has been generally thought unlucky for the prospective bride to make her own dress; in Bohemia she was said to be sewing her shroud. When the dress is being fitted, she should never look at herself in a mirror, lest something happen to prevent the marriage. When she first puts on the finished dress, which should take place as late as possible before the wedding date, her marriage will be a success if the fit is good, but she can expect sorrow and trouble if alterations are required. If a friend tries on the bride's dress, she will have to bear all the trials and ills of the bride. In China it was considered an ill omen if any friend dressed in mourning was present during a fitting.

When paying for the making of the dress, the bride should be sure that there are at least two pieces of silver money in the change, otherwise she or the dressmaker will have bad luck. If the bride's clothing is not paid for at the time of the wedding, death will come into the new home and take away the first child. If the groom pays for his bride's clothes, she will not be happy with him.

Under no circumstances must the groom see his bride in her wedding dress before she walks down the aisle of the church or until he meets her at the altar.

The bridal veil is of Near Eastern origin, being a relic of the bridal canopy held over the heads of the couple during the ceremony. Eastern marriages were almost always arranged between two families, and the bride was hidden from her future husband until the day of the wedding, when the groom unveiled her face and saw it for the first time.

The veil was also a disguise in the days when people believed in demon lovers. In ancient times people thought that an evil spirit, or demon, often sought to divert a girl's love and affection from her husband and family to himself. If there was a demon lover who desired the girl for himself, he might harm the human rival whose courtship had been successful. Therefore, it was necessary to deceive the devil, to throw him off the track, and that was the purpose of the veil—to conceal the bride's identity. Today, most brides walk to the altar with their faces covered, and the veil is raised at the end of the ceremony by the groom. In the past that was the moment when the demon lover realized he had lost the one he loved.

Only when she is on the point of leaving for the ceremony is it considered "safe" for a bride to look at herself fully clothed and veiled. This superstition stems from the old mirror belief that part of oneself goes into the reflection, and it would be a very bad start for their life together if the bride failed to give the whole of herself to her future husband. However, she can avoid losing part of herself in the mirror if she leaves off a shoe or a glove when she looks in the mirror.

The presence of the bridesmaids and/or matron of honor, as well as of the best man, is a relic of the days of capture. They are supposed to represent the friends of the two parties and prevent the possible abduction of the bride. The bridesmaids' duties are to assist the bride in dressing, accompany her to the church, and follow her down the aisle to the altar, thus protecting her from both the demon lover and any unsuccessful suitor who might at the last moment attempt to kidnap her. The matron of honor is always a married woman. Representing the happy marital state, she is assumed to bring particular good luck to the bride.

An old superstition says that a bridesmaid can expect to have the good fortune of becoming a bride within a year, and one who catches the bridal bouquet is even more sure of marrying. Woe to that bridesmaid who stumbles in the procession to the altar, for she will be doomed to become an old maid! The saying "Always a bridesmaid, never a bride" is more specific in the superstition "Thrice a bridesmaid, never a bride." Some hope is offered in the belief that she can break this jinx by being a bridesmaid seven times, a lucky number for her!

Since there can be no wedding ceremony without the

MARRIAGE

bridegroom, he might logically be expected to be the subject of at least as many superstitions as his partner. But, alas, the focus of attention is nearly always on the bride; she is the star occupying the center of the stage, while he plays a subordinate role.

According to a British superstition, if the bridal party on the way to the church meets a member of the clergy, a policeman, a doctor, a lawyer, or a blind person, bad luck is sure to follow. Seeing a funeral procession also foretold doom. It was considered most unfortunate if there was an open grave in the churchyard. If so, planks had to be placed over it. If the bridal couple entered the church by one door and went out by another, it was held to be a bad omen, too. This belief corresponds to a funeral superstition that requires the coffin to be taken into the church by a side door and out through the main (front) door.

The characterization of the wedding ceremony as "tying the knot" refers to an ancient Babylonian custom. A thread was taken from the clothes of both the bride and the bridegroom and tied together to symbolize the union.

As another symbol of the marriage union—"With this ring I thee wed"—the wedding circlet is the subject of many superstitions, with scores of special beliefs in different countries. To primitive man, it signified that the bride, who was usually captured, was bound to her husband, whose spirit would enter her body. She was thus tied to him by this "magic circle," which could never be broken. The ring would also ward off evil spirits, which might threaten the happiness of the bride. To the ancient Egyptians, the circle represented eternity, and marriage was looked upon as a permanent bond.

The ring, which originated in the East and was adopted by the Greeks and Romans, finally became a part of Christian ceremonies in the ninth century. The wedding ring constituted a strengthening of the bond of the engagement ring, and the Church considered it a sacred bond welding the couple in wedlock. The "lock" in wedlock did not refer to a lock, however; it is derived from the old English term *lác*, which could mean several different things. "Wed" meant a pledge.

The ring should always be paid for by the groom, and it should never be given to him as a gift. If the bride buys the ring, she will never live happily with her husband.

The reason for the choice of the left hand was the traditional belief that the right hand stood for power and authority (the man as master), and the left hand symbolized submission and serfdom (the wife as slave). The third finger was selected for an unusual reason, which can be tested (try it!): The third finger is the only one which cannot be freely stretched or moved independently, and a ring cannot easily slip off it.

To drop the ring before or during the wedding service was very unlucky. If either the groom or the bride dropped it, he or she would be the first to die. If it rolled away from the altar steps, the ill omen was even stronger. Today, if a young ring bearer is in the wedding party, the ring is usually stitched loosely to the small pillow he carries. Experienced clergymen, familiar with the traditional nervousness of bridegrooms, carry a duplicate so that the accident will not interrupt the ceremony.

MARRIAGE

It is still popularly held that no one but the husband should ever remove the wedding ring; taking it from a sick, dying, or dead person is bad luck, and it should always be buried with the body. If it becomes too tight, evil can be anticipated; if it breaks, death will follow.

At the end of the ceremony the groom raises his wife's veil and kisses her for the first time as her husband, thus sealing his vows and pledges before the assembled guests. A common superstition is that the bride should then cry, because if she does not, her married life will be full of tears. In Scotland the pastor used to be the first to kiss the bride, as her happiness was said to depend on his blessing.

Among Orthodox Jews it is the custom for the bridegroom to break a glass with his foot and for the entire company to cry out as loudly as possible, *"Mazel tov"* ("Good luck"). The breaking of the glass is said to commemorate the destruction of the Temple of Jerusalem by the Romans in A.D. 70, a tragedy that should be remembered even in moments of greatest joy. The custom of crushing a breakable hollow object with the foot is also practiced in the marriage ceremony of a Hindu couple.

The cake at wedding feasts and receptions has evolved over a long period of history. Among the Romans of the upper class there existed a form of marriage ceremony in which the essential feature was *confarreatio,* "eating together." Together, in the presence of ten witnesses, the bride and groom ate a special kind of cake made of wheat or barley, which was thought to guarantee both happiness and children. The cake was then broken over the bride's head and the guests picked up and ate the small pieces. A similar custom is practiced by the Iroquois Indians.

The bridecake ceremonies have varied, the food always symbolizing fertility. Guests at early Anglo-Saxon weddings brought small, dry biscuits, and after everyone had taken one, the leftovers were distributed to the poor. Later, in England, during the reign of Elizabeth I, small buns, much like modern shortbread, were thrown upon the head of the bride as she left the church, a custom that was later replaced by rice throwing. Finally, during the reign of Charles II, the many small cakes were replaced by one large cake, often in tiers and elaborately decorated.

The wedding cake should never be baked by the future bride lest bad luck follow. Nor should she taste it; if she does taste it on the night before the wedding, her husband's love will soon cease. If the groom is in the house while the cake is baking, it will fall. In Persia the dough is prepared by seven young girls of marriageable age, to ensure seven children to the couple, seven being a lucky number.

Small charms, each with its own meaning, are still often baked into the cake, and anyone who receives a slice containing one is considered fortunate. The saying goes: "If you find in your piece of wedding cake the ring, you are to marry; the thimble, you will be an old maid; the coin, you will be rich."

An unmarried girl who sleeps with a piece of the cake under her pillow is sure to dream of her future husband. A local English rhyme expresses this superstition:

> But, madam, as a present take

> This little paper of bridecake,
> In morning slumber you will seem
> To enjoy your lover in a dream.

In a variation that replaces the pillow with a stocking, the eligible girl before retiring puts her slice into a stocking together with three slips of paper on which are written the names of three young men she considers suitable marriage prospects. On the next two mornings she draws out two of the slips, and the one remaining on the third day tells her the name of the man to whom she will become betrothed and will eventually marry.

Among ancient Britons both men and women followed this custom. They would eat some of the cake and then have a vision in the night of the one they would marry. Another British belief holds that if a bride keeps a morsel of the cake in the pocket of one of her dresses until the honeymoon is over, she will still be married when the dress wears out.

Among primitive peoples flowers symbolized sex energy and were believed to be aids to fertility. The bridal bouquet was therefore intended to save the bride from barrenness and marital unhappiness. Decorated with ribbons that are tied in knots, it is said to hold the good wishes of the bride's friends. The girl who catches the bouquet when it is thrown by the bride as she sets out on her honeymoon will be the next one to be married. The lucky girl immediately makes a wish for the bride, which will come true if she also unties one of the knots; this wish should be for happiness and children for the couple. The men are not forgotten, for the bride throws her garter to the bachelors in the groom's party, and the lucky one who catches it will become the next bridegroom among them.

Rice throwing was an ancient custom in the Far East. Originally rice or grain was thrown at the newlyweds to appease the demon lover in case he had not been deceived by the bride's veil; the offering of food supposedly diverted his attention, so that he would not harm the happy couple. Later rice, the Oriental symbol of fertility, became a charm to bless the marriage with many children. Rice throwing without demon association was a part of the ancient religious rites of the Hindus and the Chinese.

Instead of rice, the ancient Romans threw nuts and sugared almonds (sweetmeats) at the bride. The word "confetti" comes from the Italian, being of the same root as the word "confectionery." As an inexpensive paper substitute for rice, confetti has taken its place in many modern weddings, often in the form of flower petals and hearts.

Folklorists, perhaps with tongue in cheek, have pointed out the incongruity of showering a couple with symbols of fertility in an age when birth control is becoming increasingly popular. Since our contemporary world is, above all, realistic, churches and clubs in the United States are starting to add a cleaning charge when rice or confetti is thrown on the property after weddings and receptions. Thus the custom may gradually be abandoned and become, like many other superstitious practices, a memory of the past.

MARRIAGE

The word "honeymoon" derives from the custom, observed in some European countries, of the newly married couple's drinking mead, a wine made of honey and water, for a month or until the next moon after marriage: Thus the word "honey" plus "moon" (month) meant the first month of marriage, which was thought of as the sweetest.

Whether the couple goes directly to their new home or enters it after the honeymoon, tradition requires that the bride be carried over the threshold for good luck. To reinforce this belief, modern bridegrooms often carry their brides into the hotel rooms on their honeymoons as well. The custom goes back to the time when wives did not go willingly into the man's house but had to be captured. A later belief of the Romans was that stumbling was a sign of bad luck. Therefore, to prevent such an accident, the cautious bridegroom carried his bride. They also believed that demons stood watch at the threshold, eager to capture her. To avoid any contact with them the young husband carried his bride across the threshold.

15. Death

"I can hardly think there was ever anyone scared into Heaven."
—Sir Thomas Browne, English physician, *Religio Medici* (1643)

"The fear of death is more to be dreaded than death itself" is as true today as when it was written in the first century B.C. by the Latin author Publilius Syrus. Death has appropriately been called "the ultimate mystery." It is an experience that must come to everyone—to one's family, one's friends, and oneself. In fact, life has been termed "a continuous progress toward death." Death is inevitable.

The mystery surrounding death puzzled the primitive savage as much as it perplexes modern man. Religion has sought to explain its meaning, so that we may be able to understand its significance and to bear our grief when a loved one dies. The seeming finality of death leads one to wonder about the secrets of a possible afterlife, so it is not surprising that beliefs concerning all aspects of dying and death have been numerous and still form a large body of contemporary superstitious lore.

The most enduring of such superstitions is that the howling of a dog at night is a sign of a death soon to come. From ancient times the dog has been credited with the power of "seeing" death when it enters a house. The belief that he sees it at night is undoubtedly due to the fact that the largest number of deaths occur during the hours of darkness, particularly those of the early morning, when the resistance of a fatally ill person is lowest.

The belief in a howling dog is particularly prevalent among Southern Negroes in the United States, as stated in the words of an elderly black woman: "Something's going to happen if a dog outside the door gets to howling—that's a sign somebody's dead, that's truly so."

Variations of this general statement are that if a dog howls persistently in front of or within a house where someone lies ill, that person will die, especially if the animal concerned belongs to him or to some other member of the household. If the wailing dog is out of doors, is driven away, and then returns to howl again, the omen is considered to be incontestable. So too, if a dog howls suddenly, one or more times, and then becomes silent, that is a sign that a death has occurred somewhere nearby. In the French version the sign portends the death of the sick person sometime during the following year.

The actions of an owl are also considered to indicate a foreboding of death. In Scotland and England particularly, an owl entering or flying around a house or perching on the roof is a death omen. Constant hooting, especially the repeated cry of the screech owl, is widely thought to indicate an impending death.

The Negro woman quoted above recited a rhyme popular among Southern blacks:

> When you hear the screech owl, honey, in the sweet gum tree,
> It's a sign as sure as you're born a death is bound to be;
> Unless you put the shovel in the fire mighty quick
> For to conjure that old screech owl, take care the one that's sick.

History records many instances where the screech owl has been regarded as having predicted the death of some prominent person. According to Shakespeare, the murder of Julius Caesar was forewarned by the screeching of an owl:

> The bird of night did sit
> E'en at noonday upon the marketplace,
> Hooting and shrieking.

Similarly, if a bird flies into a sickroom, death is sure to follow. A falling star, that hardy perennial in the store of superstitions, may also indicate that someone is dying, for the star represents the soul. Since someone dies somewhere every minute, this belief can be readily rationalized.

In the days before electricity, and currently in many rural areas, the flickering light of a candle was thought to indicate that death was near. If a candle guttered as it burned, the grease collected unevenly and gradually lengthened into a winding-sheet, or shroud; if a draft caused the flame to waver, the shroud in which the dead body would eventually be wrapped was thought to be symbolically woven. Even if no one in the family was sick when the candle guttered, a member of the household would surely become ill and finally die.

Another old-time omen, still believed among country folk, concerned bells. Their ringing in the ears was a sure sign of the nearness of death. A corresponding belief concerned the hearing of a so-called death rap. If, while the members of a family were gathered to await the imminent passing of a dying person, they heard three raps in the wall, it meant that death could be expected at any moment. In Scotland people still claim to hear these three knocks at regular intervals of one or two minutes' duration; in Germany during the *Totenwacht* (the deathwatch) the same phenomenon occurs.

The original idea behind this superstition was that the spirit of Death was knocking for admission into the sickroom. The actress Fanny Bergen, a diligent collector of American superstitions, was informed by one of those who submitted this belief that the sound was actually only the noise of two spiders, which happened to strike against each other in the wall of a room occupied by a dying person. The clicking noise of certain beetles calling to their mates was also said to cause this deathwatch sound.

Other warning omens were the breaking of a looking glass and the falling of a picture from the wall in a sickroom. In Greece if a pair of scissors is left open on a table, it is said that the Archangel Michael's mouth is open, ready to take the soul of some member of the family. Southern Negroes believe that death is near when the sick person calls for someone who is already dead.

Because the presence of death is faced by most people with fear and dread, behavior in the death chamber, superstition holds, requires that a person must never speak above a whisper, must never turn his back upon the dying, and must directly face him when leaving the room.

The actual moment of dying is the subject of many beliefs. The eyes should immediately be closed by someone present while the body is still warm. It is thought that if they are left open, the deceased person will look for someone to join him in death. A coin, which could be used in future life, was often placed on each eye. However, this act was a practical one, so that the undertaker would not have difficulty in closing the eyelids after they had stiffened. Pulling a sheet over the head is a throwback to the time when bodies were buried in shrouds rather than clothes.

An old superstition, traced to eighteenth-century Germany and still prevalent in Great Britain, held that after someone dies, the windows in the room should be opened immediately so that his soul can leave on the journey to its future home.

In European villages a church bell, called the passing bell or the soul bell, is rung when a parish member dies. Traditionally, the sound of church bells was believed to drive away demons and evil spirits, which might harm the souls and bodies of human beings. In Elizabethan England this custom was even spelled out in a royal order: "after the time of passinge, to ringe no more but one short peale."

Francis Grose, an eighteen-century English antiquarian, explained its significance:

> The passing bell was anciently rung for two purposes: one to bespeak the prayers of all good Christians for a soul just departing, the other to drive away the evil spirits at the bed's foot and about the house, ready to seize their prey or at least to molest and terrify the soul in its passage. But by the ringing of the bell, they were kept aloof, and the soul, like a hunted hare, gained the start or had what is by sportsmen called law [a chance to escape].

The passing bell thus notified the villagers of the death, "the departure of the soul," and was considered a request for the town folk to pray for the protection of the soul as it set out on its long journey into the next world.

After a death, all mirrors in the house should be covered or turned toward the wall, because whoever sees his reflection in them will die soon after, or someone else in the house will die.

There is still a widespread belief that a clock may stop at the exact time of its owner's death. So deep-rooted was this superstition in the United States during the late nineteenth century that one of the most popular songs of the 1870's was "Grandfather's Clock," by Henry Clay Work.

The several verses tell of the principal events in the old man's life from his birth, and each line is followed by "ticktock, ticktock," which adds to the song's rhythmic appeal. The final verse tells of the old man's death:

> Ninety years without slumbering,
> His life's seconds numbering,
> But it stopped short, never to go again,
> When the old man died.

If you consider the time when the song attained popularity, its ending does not seem contrived. A grandfather clock was an expensive luxury and had a delicate mechanism. It was the work of a craftsman skilled in woodworking, and because of its rarity and fragile works, only the owner wound it. This was not done when he was ill, lest the impression be given that he would not recover, so the clock ran down and inevitably stopped. Visitors to the home, noticing that time was standing still, attributed it to a supernatural power, especially if, through coincidence, it accidentally stopped at the hour of death.

Another old superstition held that all the clocks in the house should be stopped and not set in motion again until after the burial. This was to protect the living by indicating to Death that his task was done and life should take over.

Certain other actions were to be taken during the period between the time of death and the funeral. Before there were professional undertakers, the preparation of the body for burial, the washing and clothing of the corpse—the laying out—was undertaken by the family if the death occurred at home, and by nurses if in a hospital. The corpse was never left alone, locked in a room, or left in the dark. Even today in many cases candles play an important role during this time. They are relics from the days when fires were lighted around the dead to frighten away the evil spirits that wished to bear the corpse into the realms of darkness. The bier is often flanked by candles that are burned continuously, both day and night, before the funeral. The casket, formerly called a coffin, is often "watched" continuously by shifts of guards, who are usually male family members or very close friends.

The wearing of black by members of the mourning family dates back to pagan days, when it was worn as a disguise, so that the spirit of the deceased (the ghost) would not recognize them and haunt them. A modern explanation of the use of black for mourning is given by Rudolph Brasch in his book *How Did It Begin?* He calls it "a superb example of man's way to spiritualize and rationalize ancient superstitions." Black, he asserts, is symbolic of the night, "and the absence of color seemed best suited to express a person's abandonment to grief. The color of mourning also served as a constant reminder of the loss one has suffered." The wearing of a black band around a man's left coat sleeve has always been a common expression of grief in many countries.

Colors other than black are used for mourning in some countries. In Iran, for example, mourners wear sky blue to symbolize the heaven (the sky) to which the dead have departed. The Egyptian color is yellow, which shows that, even as plants and leaves are yellow when faded or dead, so is the end of human life and hope. By universal custom, many dark-skinned people use white for mourning, and whites use black. For example, in Southeast Asia, white is worn at funerals, since death is considered to be a joyful occasion for the departed, a release from his pain and suffering. The aborigines of Australia also use white, and when a close relative dies, they plaster their foreheads, the tips of their noses, and their eyelids with white pipe clay. This is done to make them invisible to Death.

The wake in the presence of the body, alternately called the watch, is a custom still followed by many Catholics, whether the body remains in the home or lies in a funeral establishment. Friends thus help the family members in "keeping company" with the dead. Candles "light the way" of the deceased. The famous traditional Irish wake was often a boisterous social occasion lasting several nights, particularly if the dead person was old. According to Arnold Dobrin, however, such noisy behavior, lacking in respect for the dead, came to be frowned upon.

> This was by no means simply a desire for festive sociability, but, according to many students of folklore, was founded in a deep and universal fear of the dead. Apparently it was thought that the dead were envious of the living, and that they would try to get an opportunity to revenge themselves on those who claimed their property.
>
> Consequently, every effort possible was made to assure the dead that the living still regarded them with sympathy and love.... The dead person was, in fact, the honored guest of the party....*

But because the Church considered that the traditional and lengthy wake had become too much of a social occasion, it is now customary for the body to remain home only one night.

In certain countries, particularly Italy, a coin is often

---

*Arnold Dobrin, in *Ireland: The Edge of Europe* (Nashville and New York, Thomas Nelson Inc., 1970), p. 143.

put into the hands or on the tongue of the dead sometime before burial, a practice that presumably comes from ancient Greece, when the souls of the dead had to cross the River Styx on their journey from the earth. Charon, the ferryman from Hades, required that the fare be paid, and so the Greeks placed a coin in the dead person's mouth for this fee, and the Romans took over this custom.

The rites connected with funerals and burials involve a few superstitions that dedicated followers still faithfully observe.

The funeral is the final public tribute to the deceased. In the United States, if the casket is open, the undertaker will, at the conclusion of the service, announce that those present may pass in front and take their last look at the face of the corpse. When they pass the casket, many elderly people touch the forehead of the dead person. According to an old superstition, this act is intended to prevent them from dreaming of the deceased or seeing him in any form, particularly as a ghost.

If the procession to the cemetery is by foot, as in small towns in Britain and in almost all of the other European countries, the members of the family are supposed to walk together first, followed by friends, because the family must remain closest to the dead person before the final separation at the grave.

If the cortege is motorized, it should never be broken into or interrupted. In modern cities the cars in a procession, generally marked by a sign on the windshields and with the lights turned on, are given the right of way and even go through red traffic lights to keep up with the hearse. In addition to showing respect for the dead, this tradition derives from the ancient belief that if the progress of the deceased to the grave is interrupted, an unhappy spirit (the corpse), reluctant to leave the familiar physical world, might take advantage of a halt by escaping from the body to haunt or harm the living.

An old superstition holds that the number of automobiles (formerly carriages) in a cortege should never be counted for either of two reasons: The number will indicate the years the person who counted has yet to live, or a death will soon occur in his family. American Negroes believe that the first person to drive a new hearse will be the one next to die.

A grave should always be dug along an east-west line, and the body placed in it so that on the day of resurrection the dead can rise facing the east, from which the call will come.

Bad luck will follow if the grave is not ready when the procession arrives, for the same reason as the taboo against interrupting a cortege.

The burial ceremony marks the last contact of the deceased with those left behind. It is therefore a very personal rite, and superstition holds that persons not belonging to the family should not be present at the grave service unless they are specifically invited. Those who intrude on this private rite may themselves die shortly. Burials of public figures, of course, are an exception.

If difficulties are encountered in lowering the casket into the grave, the soul of the dead person is thought to be making a final struggle to escape; sometimes this is interpreted as a last attempt of evil spirits to gain control of the soul.

There is a common belief in Britain and Ireland that the most recently buried corpse in a cemetery must act as the "graveyard watcher," guarding the burial ground and summoning those in the locality who are to die. The watcher is relieved of his duties when another burial occurs.

It is considered very bad luck to step on a grave at any time, because the anger of the dead might be aroused. If the earth on a new grave sinks rapidly, the dead person is thought to be making room for a surviving member of the family, and another death will be sure to take place. American Negroes say that you should always cross your fingers when passing a graveyard; if you don't, you will die.

Every country follows its own customs regarding death and the rites and beliefs associated with it. Though some are variations of the universal practices, others are unique to the locality and the beliefs concerning afterlife.

Chinese peasants continue the practice of ancestor worship and consider that their good fortune on earth depends on the favorable influence of their dead. The journey of a person to join his ancestors in the afterlife must therefore be made as easy as possible. Devils and evil spirits, which might impede his progress or harm the living, must be frightened away. The mourners put rice in the mouth of the deceased so that he or she will have food for the long journey. At the funeral they burn imitation money to pay the way of their dead to the "shady realms," and real money is buried with the corpse so that the gods will be rewarded for receiving the soul to join his ancestors.

A sedan chair is burned at the funeral of a woman so that she may be carried to paradise; men, presumably stronger, walk. To help the deceased on the trip, he is provided with a so-called bridge ladder. As a bridge it will aid him in crossing rivers, and as a ladder it will assist him in climbing mountains toward his goal. He is also supplied with a lantern to light his way into the unknown.

In funeral processions the faces of the mourners are covered to prevent them from being recognized by spirits, which might harm them. Golden paper ornaments are thrown along the route because the devil is fond of paper. Attracted by the shiny pieces, he will be too busy picking them up to interfere with the soul of the departed as it starts on its way to heaven. If, having buried the head of the family, a survivor is pursued by bad luck, it is taken as a sign that the body is dissatisfied with its resting-place.

Like the Chinese, the Koreans revere their ancestors and faithfully perform the ceremonies due the dead. The body is placed in a very thick wooden coffin so that evil spirits cannot reach it, and it is preserved many months in a room set aside for that purpose. The relatives weep only in this death chamber, and do it three or four times a day. In the funeral procession a red banner is carried to frighten away evil spirits, and the men wear hideous masks for their own protection.

In Japan when someone dies, all the screens and doors in the house are turned upside down, and all the clothing of the dead person is turned inside out, indicating his release from his earthly existence. In the past the Japanese used to burn down a dwelling where someone had died, in the belief that no one could prosper if he lived in that house. Today, however, they may build a fire in front of the entrance door and throw oils and spices into the flames to bring good luck to the remaining relatives. They place the body on the floor, but do not put a pillow under the head, lest the soul be so comfortable that it will not leave the body. An unsheathed sword is laid across the feet to keep evil spirits away. All the visiting friends offer a gift of incense and pray beside the corpse. Next to it is a small box containing a thousand peas, to be counted during the recital of the thousand prayers and invocations, which they believe will improve the condition of the soul on its journey into the unknown. Six yen coins are later placed in the coffin, one for each of the six Jigo (gods) that stand at the entrances to the six shadowy worlds through which the soul must pass.

In parts of Japan funerals are held in the evening instead of the daylight hours to avoid the evil eye, which might harm the mourners in the procession. A Japanese grave is generally eight feet deep, so that the soul, if reluctant to enter the realm of the unknown, cannot return to the world of the living. The body is buried with the head in any direction but north, which at all times is an unlucky point of the compass and from which the cold comes.

Regardless of their tribes, the North American Indians have always believed that the spirits of the dead find peace and contentment in a "happy hunting ground"—a hunting ground because their society is dominated by males, and the hunt was once their principal activity in life. The Pueblo version is that when they die, their spirits go to the "land of the hereafter," which is a place where it is always summer and abundant forests permit hunting. To be killed in battle used to be considered much more lucky than to die a natural death, because a warrior fared better in the next world.

Some Indian tribes believe that the tepee of death becomes the habitation of evil spirits, and the survivors move to another place and set up a new home. Certain Indians fear to go near the dead, because they think the spirit that killed the deceased may enter into the living and kill them as well. Since the evil spirit has more influence over children than adults, children are not permitted to participate in any of the mourning and burial rites.

While a family is in mourning, the members should not cry in the house where the death has occurred, lest the spirits attack them during this period of weakness. Widows often cut off their hair to show their love and respect, and mourn for a year. Like the ancient Egyptians, Indians universally believe that the dead should be supplied with food and other items to take with him on his journey. If the spirit has nothing to eat, it will not leave, but will stay in the house. When family members are asleep, the spirit will come and whisper that it is very hungry, and it will not leave without food. In addition to food Indians generally put in the graves of their dead hunters and warriors a pouch of tobacco, a bottle of whiskey, and their guns, to console them on their way and for them to use after they reach the happy hunting ground. During the mourning period food is regularly placed at the head of the grave.

Some Indian tribes paint the face of the corpse red so

that he will not show a pale face if he is afraid of the future. In the grave the head must face toward the east, because the spirit will rise with the sun the first morning after burial and start on its long journey. Graves are always shallow to enable the spirit to escape. The California Indians keep a watch over the graves of their dead for three days and nights. The Omaha and Winnebago maintain a fire for four days and four nights to provide light for their dead on the way to the unknown world.

The Mohawk Indians consider it bad luck to allow grass to grow upon a grave, and many tribes dig up any grass so that evil spirits will have nothing to cling to if they attempt to seize the soul of the dead person. A custom widely practiced all over the world, and followed by some Indian tribes, is to place the corpse on a platform aboveground. This is to make it easier for the soul to reach the spirit world.

The custom of refraining from all mention of the names of the dead is still widely observed among many peoples. This is true among the Australian aborigines, as well as among American Indian tribes. The principal motive for the taboo is undoubtedly the fear of calling up the ghost of the deceased. If it is absolutely necessary to make reference to one who has died, the departed one is referred to in a subdued voice as "the lost one," or "the poor fellow that is no more," so that the absent spirit will not be evoked by name.

Two special types of death, suicide and drowning, are surrounded by superstition. The Catholic Church considers suicide a mortal sin, but Christian burial is permitted because suicides are deemed to be temporarily insane. Jews bury them along the wall of the cemetery. The graves of suicides have always been avoided in the past, "lest the devil seize you." British law once required that they be buried, not in a cemetery, but at a point where four roads met, partly because of the magical power of the cross in any form, partly because of the belief that the ghost would not be able to find the right road to those he wished to haunt. A stake was driven through the body so that the spirit would be held down and therefore not disturb the living. The souls of suicides were thought to be lost, wandering aimlessly in their search for a peaceful resting-place. Seeking human companionship and sympathy, they often haunted the living.

A Hindu belief is that anyone who commits suicide is doomed to perdition, for his soul is lost. If a Chinese kills himself, it is believed that he will appear in the afterlife with the knife or whatever instrument he used to kill himself.

Death by drowning has attracted much superstitious belief, mainly because the ancient idea was that evil water deities, or sprites, caused drownings by seizing their victims. An inhuman belief, widely observed during the nineteenth century, was that one should make no attempt to save a drowning person for fear of paying the penalty of one's own death by drowning to make up for the person saved. As explained by the noted English anthropologist Sir Edward Tylor in his *Primitive Culture,* the idea behind this superstition is that when a man is drowning, it is the will and intention of the water gods, and if the rescuer is successful, he must be a substitute and be drowned himself later on. A more reasonable explanation is the fear, almost cowardice, which seizes a would-be rescuer, who realizes that a drowning person usually struggles desperately with anyone who comes near him. Also an observer sometimes becomes paralyzed at the sight of a person fighting for his life.

One of the reasons a Chinese is reluctant to save a man from drowning comes from the belief that the ghost of the last person who has died must act as a watchman in purgatory until another soul arrives to relieve him of his post. In 1970, Chinese law still forbade the rescue of a drowning person because it would interfere with his fate, and even today, the Chinese throw salt into the water where a person has drowned to appease the water gods.

The most popular unfounded belief concerning drowning is that the body rises to the surface three times before finally sinking. Drowning people often do come to the surface two, three, even more times. The body at first tends to rise to the surface because of the air in the lungs and the movement of the limbs, but frequently a drowning person sinks at once.

The unfounded belief that a dying person sees his whole life pass before him is especially thought to apply to someone who is drowning. However, people who have been rescued and revived testify that, if they thought of anything at all before lapsing into unconsciousness, it was of survival.

The problem of finding a drowned body has given rise to many superstitions. One of the most common methods was to float a loaf of bread containing quicksilver over the area; it was supposed to stop directly over the body.

Sometimes a lighted candle was attached to a board and floated in the water; the flame would presumably go out when the board passed over the corpse. An old superstition of the American Indians was that if they rowed a boat with a rooster on board around and around, the rooster would crow over the spot where the body lay.

Some traditions say that a drowned person will rise to the surface within a week. An officer of the Missing Persons Bureau of the New York City Police Department has asserted that bodies rise to the surface quicker in springtime, and that men float face down, while women float on their backs, face up.

Because of what happens after death is filled with unsolved mysteries, an entire body of superstition has seized the imagination of the living. A grave or tomb should never be disturbed, for the wrath of the dead will result in a curse that will bring all manner of bad luck and even death. In the 1920's a party of English archaeologists entered the sealed tomb of the ancient Egyptian king Tutankhamen in the Valley of the Tombs near Luxor and removed the mummy and artifacts. The widely publicized curse of the long-dead king proved to be thoroughly effective, for all who took an active part in the dismantling of the tomb died one by one.

The folklore surrounding belief in ghosts is so extensive that full-length books have been written on the subject. Even today the idea of being haunted is very real among country folk. Although the five thousand readers of the *People* that Geoffrey Gorer surveyed were generally uncertain of such beliefs, a fair percentage admitted to full or partial belief. Two questions were asked and answered:

Do you believe in ghosts?

Yes 17%, No 58%, Uncertain 23%, No opinion 2%

If you believe in ghosts, have you ever seen one? (Asked of the eight hundred who answered Yes.)

Yes 42%, No 22%, Uncertain 35%, No opinion 1%

These people obviously felt that there was some truth to the belief that spirits return to haunt us.

Behind all the beliefs surrounding death and burial is the inescapable fact that death is the final experience of every single individual. From the beginning man has felt that supernatural beings and the forces of nature influenced human life for good or ill. According to Philip Waterman in *The Story of Superstition,* "Human beings often appear to be mere pawns in the hands of supernatural forces, most of which are jealous of us and seek to impose upon us all sorts of unhappiness. These are the powers of darkness and destruction; they are the hosts of Death."

The belief in luck is nothing more than wishing that good things will happen to bring us love and happiness, success and contentment, so that we can live a good life instead of suffering an unhappy, miserable existence.

Whether their lives have been happy or unhappy, however, men have seen in death a second chance at happiness, to be attained in an unknown future life. It is no wonder, then, that they have always feared and been fascinated by this greatest of enigmas.

Appendix

PERCENTAGES OF YES ANSWERS IN SELECTED STUDIES*

	1 (200)	2 (950)	3 (550)	4 (875)	5 (557)	6 (350)	7 (186)
1. New moon		12	4	9	54		
2. Finding a pin		13	8				24
3. Wearing or carrying a charm		24					
4. Rabbit's foot		31			65		
5. Four-leaf clover	38	64	26		64		
6. Horseshoe	21	56		5	67		
7. Horseshoe over door		39					
8. Seven		27			48		
9. Three		17	3				
10. Birthday slap on back		48					
11. Thirteen		15	13	14	64	30	

*See Chapter 3 and page 197. Figures in parentheses indicate number of persons questioned in studies.

APPENDIX

		1	2	3	4	5	6	7
12.	Thirteen at table		12			32		
13.	Friday the thirteenth		18	7	14	56		
14.	Walking under ladder		28	7		58		
15.	Opening umbrella		33					
16.	Breaking mirror	25	33	3		61		
17.	Black cat		40	9				
18.	Three cigarettes		16			45		
19.	Spilling salt		34					
20.	In and out of bed		23			59		
21.	Sneezing		10					
22.	Knock on wood		55	31		64		58
23.	Wish on first star	51	40	4		54		54
24.	Wish on falling star		28					
25.	Wishbone		43	5		69		

Sources and Readings

The author is grateful to the authors and publishers of the works listed below for information and both quoted and unquoted material. Authors have been indicated in the text only when direct quotations have been used. The following bibliography is limited for the most part to materials published since 1930, either in original or reprint form. There are, of course, many valuable studies of earlier date.

BOOKS

Bauer, William W., *Potions, Remedies and Old Wives' Tales.* New York, Doubleday, 1969.

Benninger, John A., *Superstitions and American Folklore.* Louisville, Kentucky, Cardinal Publishing Co., 1932. Reprint: Detroit, Gale Research Co.

Bergen, Fanny D., ed., *Current Superstitions, Collected from the Oral Tradition of English-Speaking Folk* (Published for the American Folklore Society). Boston, Houghton Mifflin, 1896. Reprint: New York, Kraus Reprint Co., 1969.

Brasch, Rudolph, *How Did It Begin? Customs and Superstitions and Their Romantic Origins.* London, Longmans, 1965; New York, McKay, 1966. Paperback: New York, Pocket Books, 1969.

Brelsford, Vernon, *Superstitious Survivals.* London, Centaur Press, 1958; New York, McBride, 1959.

Brown, Raymond L., *A Book of Superstitions.* Newton Abbot, England, David & Charles, 1970; New York, Taplinger, 1970.

Budge, Sir Ernest A. T. W., *Amulets and Superstition.* London, Oxford University Press, 1930; New Hyde Park, New York, University Books, 1961. Reprint: New York, Collier Books, 1970.

Caldwell, Otis W., and Gerhard Lundeen, *Do You Believe It? Curious Habits and Strange Beliefs of Civilized Man.* Garden City, New York, Garden City Publishing Co., 1937. Reprint: Detroit, Gale Research Co.

Chaundler, Christine, *Everyman's Book of Superstitions.* Oxford, A. R. Mowbray & Co., 1970; New York, Philosophical Library, 1971.

Cowan, Lore, *Are You Superstitious? London, Leslie Frewen, 1968;*

Princeton, New Jersey, Brandon/Systems Press, 1969 (Apex Book). Paperback: New York, Pocket Books, 1970.

Deerforth, Daniel, *Knock Wood: Superstition Through the Ages.* New York, Brentano's, 1928. Reprint: Detroit, Gale Research Co.

Elworthy, Frederick, *The Evil Eye: The Origins and Practices of Superstition.* London, John Murray, 1895; New York, Julian Press, 1958. Paperback: New York, Macmillan, 1970 (Collier Books).

Emrich, Duncan, *Folklore of Love and Courtship.* New York, McGraw-Hill, 1970.

——. *Folklore of Weddings and Marriage.* New York, McGraw-Hill, 1970.

Evans, Bergen, *The Natural History of Nonsense.* New York, Knopf, 1946.

Fielding, William J., *Strange Customs of Courtship and Marriage.* Philadelphia, Blakiston, 1942 (Circle Books).

——, *Strange Superstitions and Magical Practices.* Philadelphia, Blakiston, 1945 (Circle Books).

Fishbein, Morris, *Shattering Health Superstitions.* New York, Liveright, 1930.

Frazer, Sir James G., *The New Golden Bough.* New York, Macmillan, 1951.

——, *Psyche's Task: A Discourse Concerning the Influence of Superstition on the Growth of Institutions.* 2d ed., rev. and enl. London, Dawsons, 1968.

Freedland, Nat., *The Occult Explosion.* New York, Putnam's, 1972.

Gibson, Walter B., and Litzka R., *The Complete Illustrated Book of the Psychic Sciences.* New York, Doubleday, 1966. Paperback: New York, Pocket Books, 1968.

Goodwin, John, *Occult America.* New York, Doubleday, 1972.

Grimm, Jakob, *Teutonic Mythology,* translated from the 4th ed. by James S. Stollybrass. 4 vols. Reprint: New York, Dover Publications, 1966. Appendix, Vol. 4, pp. 1737–1848.

Haggard, Howard W., *Mystery, Magic, and Medicine.* Garden City, New York, Doubleday, Doran, 1933.

Hand, Wayland D., "The Fear of the Gods: Superstition and Popular Beliefs." In Coffin, Tristram P., ed. *Our Living Traditions.* New York, Basic Books, 1968. pp. 215–227.

Hill, Douglas A., Magic and Superstition. London, Paul Hamlyn, 1968.

—— and Pat Williams, *The Supernatural.* London, Aldus Books,

1965; New York, Hawthorn, 1966. Paperback: New York, New American Library, 1967.

Igglesden, Sir Charles, *Those Superstitions*. London, Jarrolds, 1931. Reprint: Detroit, Gryphon Books, 1971.

Jahoda, Gustav, *The Psychology of Superstition*. London, Allen Lane, 1969. Paperback: Baltimore, Penguin Books, 1971 (Pelican Paperback).

Johnson, Clifton, *What They Say in New England and Other American Folklore*. New York, Columbia University Press, 1963.

Jones, William, *Credulities Past and Present*. London, Chatto & Windus, 1880. Reprint: Detroit, Singing Tree Press, 1968.

Lings, Martin, *Ancient Beliefs and Modern Superstitions*. London, Tomorrow Publications, 1964 (Perennial Books). U.S. edition: New York, Samuel Weiser.

Lys, Claudia de, *A Treasury of American Superstitions*. New York, Philosophical Library, 1948.

Maple, Eric, *Superstition and the Superstitious*. London, W. H. Allen, 1971. U.S. edition: Cranbury, New Jersey, A. S. Barnes and Co.

Montagu, Ashley, and Edward Darling, *The Prevalence of Nonsense*. New York, Harper & Row, 1967.

Palmer, Geoffrey, and Noel Lloyd, *Exploring Superstitions*. London, Odhams, 1967.

Parker, Derek, *Astrology in the Modern World*. New York, Taplinger, 1970.

Platt, Charles, *Popular Superstitions*. London, Herbert Jenkins, Ltd., 1925. Reprint: Detroit, Gale Research Co.

Read, Carveth A., *Man and His Superstitions*. Cambridge, England, Cambridge University Press, 1925. U.S. edition: New York, Macmillan.

Redgrove, H. Stanley, *By-gone Beliefs*. London, William Rider & Sons, 1920.

Thomen, August A., *Doctors Don't Believe It—Why Should You?* New York, Simon & Schuster, 1941. Also printed privately under title *Don't Believe It!* 1935.

Trachtenberg, Joshua, *Jewish Magic and Superstition*. New York, Behrman, 1939. Paperback: New York, Atheneum, 1970 (Temple Books).

Waterman, Philip F., *The Story of Superstition*. New York, Grosset & Dunlap, 1929. Reprint: New York, AMS Press, 1970.
Wiggam, Albert F., *Sorry, But You're Wrong About It*. Indianapolis, Bobbs-Merrill, 1931. Excerpts, *Readers Digest*, Vol. 28 (February, 1931), pp. 28-30.
Woodin, G. B., *Popular Superstitions*. Mt. Vernon, N.Y., Peter Pauper Press, 1970.

DICTIONARIES, ENCYCLOPEDIAS, AND REFERENCE WORKS

Bonnerjea, Biren, *A Dictionary of Superstitions and Mythology*. London, Folk Press, 1969. Reprint: Detroit, Singing Tree Press, 1970.
Brewer, Ebenezer C., *Brewer's Dictionary of Phrase and Fable*. 10th ed. New York, Harper & Row, 1964; London, Cassell, 1970.
Daniels, Cora L., and C. M. Stevens, *Encyclopedia of Superstitions, Folklore and Occult Sciences of the World*. 3 vols. Chicago, Yewdale & Sons Co., 1903. Reprint: Detroit, Gale Research Co., 1971.
Ferm, Vergilius, *A Brief Dictionary of American Superstitions*. New York, Philosophical Library, 1959.
Radford, Edwin, and Mona A., *Encyclopaedia of Superstitions*. 2d ed., enl. and rev. by Christine Hole. London, Hutchinson, 1961. Reprint: Chester Springs, Pa., Dufour Editions, 1969.
Stimpson, George W., *A Book About a Thousand Things*. New York, Harper & Bros., 1946.
U.S. Library of Congress, Division of Bibliography. "A Short List of References on Superstitions." 1924 (Select List of References, No. 856).
Walsh, William S., *Curiosities of Popular Customs*. Philadelphia, Lippincott, 1898. Reprint: Detroit, Gale Research Co., 1966.

JUVENILE BOOKS

Batchelor, Julie F., and Claudia de Lys, *Superstitious? Here's Why!* New York, Harcourt, Brace, 1954 (Paperback, Voyager Books); London, Collins, 1969. Grades 5-9.
Cohen, Daniel, *Superstitions*. New York, Creative Education Press, 1971. Grades 6-9.
Leach, Maria, *The Luck Book*. Cleveland, World Publishing Co., 1964. Grades 3-6.

PERIODICAL ARTICLES

Articles may be found under the general heading "Superstition" and other headings for individual subjects such as amulets, evil eye, omens, etc., in the following sources:

International Index to Periodicals, 1907-March, 1965; title changed to *Social Sciences and Humanities Index,* April, 1965-date (United States)

Readers Guide to Periodical Literature, 1900-date (United States)

Subject Index to Periodicals, 1915-1961, continued by *British Humanities Index,* 1962-date (Great Britain)

Numerous articles on superstitions in specialized localities may be found in the *Journal of American Folklore* (American Folklore Society) and *Folk-lore,* published by the Folk-lore Society (London).

"Astrology: Fad and Phenomenon." *Time,* Vol. 93 (March 21, 1969), pp. 47-56.

Battista, O. A., "How Superstitious Are You? *American Mercury,* Vol. 79 (October, 1954), pp. 118-120.

Brinton, Daniel G., "Popular Superstitions of Europe." *Century,* Vol. 56 (New Series Vol. 34; September, 1898), pp. 634-655.

Bruce, H. Addington, "Our Superstitions." *Outlook,* Vol. 98 (August 28, 1911), pp. 999-1006.

Dowman, James, "Superstitions of the Scot." *Westminster Review,* Vol. 153 (January, 1900), pp. 61-72.

Edman, Irwin, "We Superstitious Moderns." *Century,* Vol. 108 (June, 1924), pp. 188-195. Also in his *Uses of Philosophy.* New York, Simon & Schuster, 1955. pp. 87-93.

Evans, Bergen, "A Capsule History of American Superstitions." *Holiday,* Vol. 32 (July, 1962), pp. 58-59.

———, "Don't Believe All You Hear." *Atlantic,* Vol. 177 (April, 1946), pp. 71-75.

———, "The Skeptic's Corner," monthly series on unfounded beliefs. *American Mercury,* Vols. 64-71 (February, 1947-October, 1950).

"Fallacies and Superstitions," *Edinburgh Review,* Vol. 210 (July, 1909), pp. 106-133.

Fielding, William J., "Why We're Superstitious." *Science Digest,* Vol. 20 (September, 1946), pp. 85-90.

Frazer, Sir James G., "Some Popular Superstitions of the Ancients." *Folk-lore,* Vol. 1 (1890), pp. 145-171. Also in his *Garnered Sheaves.* New York, Macmillan, 1931, pp. 128-150.

Lys, Claudia de, "Superstitions, New and Old." *Science Digest,* Vol. 26 (August, 1949), pp. 17-21.

Robinson, Charles F., "Some Psychological Elements in Famous Superstitions." *American Journal of Religion and Psychology,* Vol. 1 (1905), pp. 248-267.

Taves, Isabella, "Astrology: Fun, Fraud or Key-hole to the Future?" *Look,* Vol. 33 (May 13, 1969), pp. 96-98.

"That Old Black Magic; Time Essay." *Time,* Vol. 92 (September 27, 1968), p. 42.

Winchester, James H., "I'm Not Superstitious, But ..." *Reader's Digest,* Vol. 98 (February, 1971), pp. 21-24.

STUDIES

Belanger, Agnes F., "Empirical Study of Superstitions and Unfounded Beliefs." *Iowa Academy of Science Proceedings,* Vol. 51 (1944), pp. 355-359 (200 Iowa State College students). Study No. 1.

Caldwell, Otis W., and Gerhard Lundeen, *Do You Believe It?* Garden City, New York, Doubleday, Doran, 1934 (950 junior high school students). Study No. 2.

Conklin, Edmund S., "Superstitious Belief and Practices Among College Students." *American Journal of Psychology,* Vol. 30 (January, 1919), pp. 83-103 (550 University of Oregon students). Study No. 3.

Dresslar, Fletcher B., *Superstition and Education.* Berkeley, California, University of California Press, 1907 (University of California Publications in Education, Vol. 5, No. 1; 875 California teachers college students). Study No. 4.

Gorer, Geoffrey, *Exploring English Character.* London, Barrie & Jenkins, 1955. pp. 263-270, 461-481 (*tables*). Also New York, Criterion Books, 1955.

Lundeen, Gerhard, and Otis W. Caldwell, "A Study of Unfounded Beliefs Among High School Seniors." *Journal of Educational Research,* Vol. 22 (November, 1930), pp. 257-273. A survey of studies.

Maller, Julius B., and Gerhard Lundeen, "Sources of Superstitious Beliefs." *Journal of Educational Research,* Vol. 26 (January, 1933), pp. 321-343 (557 Columbia University extension students). Study No. 5.

Nixon, Howard K., "Popular Answers to Some Psychological Questions." *American Journal of Psychology,* Vol. 36 (July, 1925), pp. 418-424 (350 Columbia University psychology students). Study No. 6.

Wagner, Mazie, "Superstitions and Their Social and Psychological Correlations Among College Students." *Journal of Educational Psychology,* Vol. 2 (January, 1928), pp. 26-37 (186 college freshmen). Study No. 7.

Index

Accidents, 59-60
Actors and actresses, 59; *see also* Theater
Addison, Joseph, quoted, 14-15
Albatross, 129-130
Alchemy, 106, 152
Alexander III, czar of Russia, 30
Alfred the Great, 24-25
American Medical Association, Journal of the, 52
Amulets, *see* Talismans and amulets
Animals, 111-112, 148
Ant, 112
Apochrypha, quoted, 98
Apple, 146
Aquarius, Age of, 106-107
Arthritis, 38, 112, 138
Asafetida, 137
Astrology, 30-31, 32, 104-107; horoscopes, 12, 25, 35, 105, 106
Astronomy, 106
Australia, 178
Austria, 55-56, 125
Authors, superstitions of, 29-30
Auto racing, 79

Bacon, Francis, quoted, 13, 64
Baseball, 72-76
Bed, wrong side of, 35, 44, 190
Belief in superstition: attitudes toward and critisms of, 12-21; education and, 36, 40-41; effect of environment on, 38-39; intelligence and, 40-41; of noted people, 22-33; reasons for, 11-12; ridicule of, 16-18; sex differences in, 39-40; studies of belief and nonbelief, 35-42, 197; tenacity of, 9-21; test for, 42-44, 190-191
Bells, 119; death, 173, 174-175
Betting, *see* Gambling
Bible, quoted, 82, 109-110
Birds, 112, 147-148, 160, 172; sea, 129-130
Birthday, 158; candles on cake, 43, 62, 190
Bishop Otter College, 58-59
Bismarck, Prince Otto von, 28
Blaine, James, 28
Body features, 45-47
Bohemia, 160
Boxing, 62, 76-78
Brand, Charles, 55
Brasch, Rudolph, quoted, 177
Bride: bouquet, 162, 167-168; captured, 161-162, 169; veil, 161-162, 165; wedding dress, 56, 158-161; *see also* Wedding
Bridegroom, 161, 162, 163, 164, 165; carrying bride over threshold, 169
Bridge, game of, 42, 69
Brooms, 56
Browne, Sir Thomas, quoted, 170
Bruce, H. Addington, 40-41
Burke, Edmund, quoted, 16
Burton, Richard, quoted, 133
Byron, Lord, 30

Caesar, Julius, 24, 105, 172

INDEX

Caldwell, Otis W., 36, 38-39, 53, 197; quoted, 11-12
Candlemas Day, 113
Candles, 18, 88, 149-150; on birthday cake, 43, 62, 190; death, 172-173, 176-177
Card playing, 42, 63, 68-70
Caribbean islands, 39, 62
Carlisle, John, 29
Cartomancy, 100-101
Caruso, Enrico, 96
Cat, black: lucky, 83, 128; unlucky, 18, 43, 95, 190
Caterpillar, woolly bear, 116-117
Charles VI, king of France, 68, 100; opera, 96-97
Charms, 9, 12, 37-38, 39, 43, 54-55, 63, 76-77, 78, 166, 190; love, 143-146; *see also* Talismans and amulets
Children: and infants, false beliefs concerning, 50-51, 135; superstitions of, 14, 34, 36-38
Chimney sweep, 55-57
China, 101-102, 123, 160-161, 168, 181-182, 186, 187
Christian Century, quoted, 21
Churchill, Winston, 32-33; quoted, 24-25
Cicero, quoted, 9
Cigarette, lighting three on a match, 18, 44, 60, 190
Clark, J. B. M., quoted, 72
Claudius, Roman emperor, 24, 147
Clocks, 19, 150; and death, 175-176
Clover, four-leaf, 43, 54-55, 190
Coincidence, 12, 26
Coins, 62, 64, 101-102, 103, 140, 161, 166, 174, 179
Colds, 134, 135, 137-138

Coleridge, Samuel Taylor, 129-130
Colors, 85, 148; mourning, 160, 177-178; wedding dress, 56, 158-161
Conklin, Edmund, 36, 39, 197
Cooper, James Fenimore, quoted, 123
Courtship and engagement, 147, 149-153
Covent Garden Theatre, London, 89-90
Cricket, 15
Cromwell, Oliver, 121
Crossed eyes, 16-17, 66, 73
Curran, C. H., 116
Crystallomancy (crystal gazing), 103
Curses, 62-63

Days, 20, 61; wedding, 156-158; *see also* Specific days
Death, 160, 161, 170-189; actions following, 174-177; approach of, 171-174; mourning period, 176-179, 184-185; rites in foreign countries, 181-185; at sea, 127-128; wake, 178-179; *see also* Funeral
Demons, evil, 19, 22, 108, 120, 174, 181; lover, 161-162, 169
Dempsey, Jack, 76-77
Dice, 62, 63, 65-66, 77, 102
Divination, 23, 26-27
Dog, 75, 111; howling, 171
Dreams, 87, 143, 144-146, 167, 179
Dresslar, Fletcher B., 35-36, 40-41, 197; quoted, 41
Drowning, 185-188
Durocher, Leo, 73

Egypt, 23, 63, 105, 164, 177, 184; royal tombs, 27, 188
England, 11, 38, 55–57, 63, 119, 166
Engleman, Edgar, 141
Evil eye, 17, 31, 39, 85, 95, 183
Eye, 135, 174; buckeye, 138

Flags, 25
Flowers, 84–85, 95, 142, 148, 149, 167; bridal bouquet, 162, 167–168
Flying Dutchman, 130–131
Folger, Charles, 29
Football, 78
Forrest, Edwin, 90–93
Fortune-telling, 23–24, 25, 39, 98–107
France, 63, 65, 68, 96–97, 100, 172
Franklin, Benjamin, 119; quoted, 154
Frazer, Sir James, 117–118; quoted, 117
Friday, 152, 157; unlucky, 17–18, 30, 33, 61, 125–127, 190
Funeral, 179–181, 183; burial and grave, 163, 180–181, 183, 184–185; procession, 163, 179–180, 182

Gambling, 56, 63–70
Gans, Joe, 77
Germany, 11, 54, 55–56, 61, 140, 173, 174
Ghosts, 13, 29, 179, 185, 188–189
Gibbons, Thomas, quoted, 129
Gloomy Sunday, song, 95
Gods and goddesses, 23–24; Greek, 121, 124, 147; Norse, 121; Roman, 118, 121, 124, 147, 155–156
Golf, 79–80
Gorer, Geoffrey, 99, 188–189

Gould, Russell, 36, 38, 197
Grant, Ulysses S., 29
Grave, *see* Funeral
Greece, 125, 174; ancient, 23, 62, 105, 118, 123–124, 164, 179
Grose, Francis, quoted, 175
Groundhog Day, 113–115, 117
Gunther, Max, 106
Gypsies, 100, 103

Haggard, H. W., quoted, 136
Hair, 51–52, 153; pins, 73; red, 66, 73
Hall, Franklin, 49
Hand, Wayland D., 11
Hands, 46; *see also* Palmistry
Hat on bed, 77
Haydn, Franz Joseph, 93
Heart: in cards, 68, 71; crossing, 34
Hiccups, 135, 140–141
Hitler, Adolf, 32–33
Horse, 111; white, 61–62
Horse racing, 78; gambling and, 56, 64, 66–68
Horseshoe, 43, 64, 190
House, leaving, 28–29, 30, 58
Humbert I, king of Italy, 31
Hunchback, 64–65, 74–75

I Ching (Book of Changes), 101–102
India, 11, 102; Hindus, 165, 168, 186
Indians, American, 166, 188; death ceremonies, 183–185
Insects, 112
Iran, 177
Ireland, 54, 181
Irving, Washington, quoted, 13–14
Italy, 11, 63, 125, 137, 179

INDEX

Japan, 11, 19-20, 119, 159, 182-183
Jarvis, D. C., 134, 138
Java, 118
Jensen, Arthur, 49
Jews, 165, 186
Jinxes, 59-60, 83, 124-125, 127
Johnson, Jack, 77
Johnson, Samuel, 30
June, 155-156

Katz, Irwin, 50
Keats, John, 144
Keller, Albert G., quoted, 20
Kemble family, 89-90
Kissing, 149, 165
Knife, 58; and fork, crossing of, 15, 16
Knots, 144-145, 149, 163, 167-168
Korea, 182

Ladder, walking under, 16, 18, 29, 43, 58-59, 190
Langford, Sam, 77
Lewis, Joseph, quoted, 71
Lightning, 24, 118-121
Lincoln, Abraham, death of, 19
Livy, quoted, 45
London Thirteen Club, 16-17
Lotteries, 64
Louis, Joe, 78
Love, 68, 142-153; charms, 143-146, 167; letters, 150-151; *see also* Courtship and engagement
Luck, 12; amulets worn for, 27, 29, 31, 43, 71, 77, 78, 79, 136-137, 190 (*see also* Rabbit foot); bad, 57-60; belief in, 53-76, 189; charms to bring, 12, 37-38, 39, 43, 54-55, 63, 76-77, 78, 143-146, 166, 190 (*see also* Clover, four-leaf); *see also* Gambling
Lundeen, Gerhard, 36-37, 38-39, 53, 197
Lys, Claudia de, 66; quoted, 64

Macbeth (Shakespeare), 88-93
McGraw, John, 75-76
Macready, William, 90-93
Madstone, 135
Magic, 10, 12, 23, 78, 94-95, 133, 134-135, 136, 149
Maller, Julius, 36-37, 197
Man, primitive, 10, 11-12, 22-23, 108, 117, 118, 121, 149, 163, 170
Marriage, *see* Wedding
Mathewson, Christopher (Christy), 71-72; quoted, 72
Matsoukas, Nick, 17
May, 156
Mead, Margaret, quoted, 22
Medicine, folk, 38, 112, 133-141
Méneval, Baron de, quoted, 25
Mesopotamia, 23, 105
Middle Ages, 106, 139, 147
Milne, A. A., quoted, 22
Mirror, 143,; breaking of, 16, 18, 34, 43, 173, 190; looking into, 86, 162, 175
Monday, 61, 152, 156, 157
Months, wedding, 155-156
Moon, 110, 113, 134, 135; honeymoon, 169; new, 43, 190
Music and musicians, 93-97
Muszaffar-ed-Din, Shah of Persia, 31

Napoleon Bonaparte, 25-27, 28
National Committee of Thirteen Against Superstition (U.S.), 17-18

Navy, British, 125, 126–127
Negroes: as baseball mascots, 74; false beliefs concerning, 47–49; superstitions of, 39, 157, 171, 172, 174, 180, 181
New Guinea, 118
Newsweek, study of Negroes, 47–48
Nicholas II, czar of Russia, 30–31
Nixon, Howard, 39, 197
Numbers, 60–61, 67; *see also* specific numbers

Omens, 14, 15, 23–24, 27, 72, 128–130, 131, 164; death, 171–174
Opal, 58
Opie, Iona and Peter, 37–38
Ovid, Roman poet, quoted, 156
Owl, 15, 122, 172

Paganini, Niccolò, 94
Palmistry, 46, 103–104
Pavement, cracks in, 30
Peacock feathers, 16, 85, 95
People, The (newspaper), 99, 188–189
Persia, 31, 166
Philip, Prince, 57
Phillips, George L., 56
Phrenology, 46
Pin, 67, 69, 144, 149–150, 159; finding of, 43, 190
Playing cards, 68–69, 100, 129; suits, 68, 101; tarot, 100–101; *see also* Cartomancy

Plenderleath, W. C., 115–116
Pliny, Roman writer, 62
Poker, game of, 69
Presentiments, 27
Publilius Syrus, quoted, 170

Quarrels, 58, 88

Rabbit foot, 18, 43, 55, 64, 77, 87, 190
Rain, 110–113, 158; rain-making, 117
Ramala, 102
Rapp, Jean, quoted, 26
Rat, 128
Redgrove, H. Stanley, quoted, 133
Religion: criticism of superstition, 19; death and, 170–171; superstition and, 10–11
Rheumatism, 112, 138–139
Rice, 168, 181; throwing of at weddings, 57, 168
Righter, Carroll, 106
Rime of the Ancient Mariner (Coleridge), 129–130
Rings, 58, 93; engagement, 152–153; wedding, 58, 163–165
Romans, 23, 105, 118, 123–124, 155–156, 164, 165, 168, 169, 179
Royalty, superstitions of, 23–24, 30–31
Russia, 30–31, 61
Ruth, Babe, 74

Sailors, 108, 123, 124; *see also* Sea
St. Agnes' Eve, 144–145
St. Christopher, 21
St. Elmo's fire, 131–132
St. Faith's Day, 145–146
St. Swithin's Day, 113, 115–116
St. Valentine's Day, 147–149
Salt, spilling of, 15, 17, 44, 190
Saturday, 61, 152, 157, 158
Schmeling, Max, 77
Schönberg, Arnold, 93
Schumann, Clara, 94
Scientific American, 125–126
Scotland, 11, 36, 53, 79–80, 160, 165, 172, 173

INDEX

Sea, 122-132; *see also* Sailors
Seven, lucky number, 43, 61, 66, 76, 190
Sex differences, 47
Shakespeare, William, 30; quoted, 53, 98, 172
Shark, 127
Ships: ghost, 130-131; launching, 123-124
Shoes, 57, 78, 86, 103, 143, 151, 162
Siddons, Sarah, 89-90
Silence, sudden, 18-19
Sky, 109-110, 177
Snake, 118, 135; bite, 136
Sneezing, 44, 129, 191
Soccer, 78
Soldiers, 21
Soothsayers, 23, 30-31, 32
Sorcery, 23, 25
Souls of dead, 129, 174, 175, 180-181, 183-185
Southerners, American, 38, 136-137, 143
Space program, U.S., 20-21, 61
Spain, 125
Spells, 39, 62; love, 143-146
Spider, 58, 173
Spirits: death and, 174, 177, 181, 184; evil, 22, 39, 64-65, 87; sea, 123-124
Spiritualists, 30-31, 39
Spitting, 62, 78
Sports, 71-81
Star: falling, 15, 44, 62, 172, 191; lucky, 25-26, 32; wishing on, 44, 62, 191
Statesmen and politicians, superstitions of, 28-29
Stevens, Thaddeus, 28
Storms, 109-110, 119, 121, 130, 131, 132, 158
String, 139-140

Stumbling, 58, 162, 169
Suicide, 185-186
Sullivan, John L., 77
Sun, 109, 110-111, 158
Sunday, 61, 125, 156, 157
Superstition, definitions of, 10-11, 20
Superstitions, most popular, 41-44, 190-191

Taboos, 85, 124, 136, 160, 185
Tales of Hoffman, opera, 96
Talismans and amulets, 27, 29, 31, 43, 71, 77, 78, 136-137, 190
Tarot, 100-101
Tartini, Giuseppe, 94-95
Taylor, Jeremy, quoted, 122
Teacup reading (Tasseography), 102-103
Terman, Lewis, 51
Theater, 82-93
Thirteen: date, 28, 61; at dinner table, 28, 32, 43, 190; Friday, 17-18, 33; unlucky, 16-18, 32, 43, 60-61, 78, 84, 86, 93, 125-126, 190
Thompson, Charles S., quoted, 34
Three: lucky, 29, 43, 60, 190; unlucky, 60
Thunder, 121; thunderstorms, 119
Thursday, 61, 152, 156-157
Times (London), 17
Toothache, 139
Trees, 150, 172
Tuesday, 61, 152, 156, 157
Tunney, Gene, 77
Two-dollar bill, 67-68
Tylor, Sir Edward, 186-187

Umbrella, 128; opened indoors, 18, 43, 190
Unfounded beliefs, 45-52

Vikings, 24-25, 123
Voodooism, 9, 39, 62, 136

Wagner, Richard, 93
Walcott, Joe, 77
Wales, 121
Walking, 58
War, 24-26
Warts, 135, 139-140
Waterman, Philip, quoted, 189
Weather, 10, 39, 108-120; forecasting, 113-117; wedding day, 158
Wedding, 154-169; bridesmaids and matron of honor, 162-163; cake, 165-167; ceremony, 161-162, 163-165; honeymoon, 169; month and day of, 155-158; rice and confetti throwing, 56, 168; sweep's luck at, 56-57; *see also* Bride; Bridegroom
Wednesday, 61, 152, 156, 157
Whistling, 78, 85-86, 95; at sea, 129
Wilde, Oscar, quoted, 16
Wilson, Woodrow, 31-32
Wind, 25, 109, 129
Wishbone, 15, 44, 191
Wishes, 62-63
Witchcraft, 9, 23, 118
Wolseley, Lord, quoted, 29
Woman's Home Companion, 41-42
Women, 69, 124, 155
Wood, knocking on, 34, 42, 44, 191
Wordsworth, William, quoted, 108
Work, Henry Clay, 175-176